RECLAIMING CHILDHOOD

Children are cooped up, passive, apathetic and corrupted by commerce ... or so we are told.

Reclaiming Childhood confronts the dangerous myths spun today about childhood. Yes, modern children are losing out on many experiences past generations took for granted, but their lives have improved in so many other ways.

Helene Guldberg exposes the stark consequences on child development of both our low expectations of fellow human beings and our safety-obsessed culture. She argues that, rather than projecting fears and uncertainties on to children, we need to allow them to grow and flourish, to balance sensible guidance with youthful independence.

Reclaiming Childhood suggests ways we can work to improve a child's experience, as well as that of parents, teachers and 'strangers', simply by taking a step back from panic and doom-mongering.

Helene Guldberg is co-founder and Director of *spiked*, the first custombuilt online current affairs publication in the UK. She teaches undergraduate and postgraduate courses in developmental psychology with the Open University and the US study abroad centres CAPA and IES.

RECLAIMING CHILDHOOD

Freedom and play in an age of fear

Helene Guldberg

Routledge
Taylor & Francis Group

LONDON AND NEW YORK

First published 2009
by Routledge
2 Park Square, Milton Park, Abingdon, Oxon OX14 4RN

Simultaneously published in the USA and Canada
by Routledge
711 Third Ave, New York, NY 10017

Routledge is an imprint of the Taylor & Francis Group, an informa business

© 2009 Helene Guldberg

Typeset in Sabon by
Taylor & Francis Books

British Library Cataloguing in Publication Data
A catalogue record for this book is available from the British Library

Library of Congress Cataloging in Publication Data
Guldberg, Helene.
    Reclaiming childhood : freedom and play in an age of fear / Helene Guldberg.
        p. cm.
    Includes bibliographical references.
    1. Child rearing. 2. Child development. I. Title.
    HQ769.G94 2009
305.23–dc22   2008028348

ISBN 978-0-415-47722-2 (hbk)
ISBN 978-0-415-47723-9 (pbk)

In loving memory of three exceptional women:
my mother, Rathie,
mother-in-law, Josephine, and
dear friend, Gina

CONTENTS

Acknowledgements   ix

Introduction   1

PART I
The good, the bad, and the history: a balance sheet of
modern childhood   5

1   A childish panic about the next generation   7

2   Cocooning children   32

3   Childhood in historical perspective   46

PART II
Freedom and child development   57

4   Growing up: why risk-taking is good for kids   59

5   Play: what is it good for?   73

6   The bullying bandwagon   92

7   Virtual lives? Media, brands and the MySpace generation   111

PART III
Taking real responsibility: the role of adult society   127

8   Let parents be parents: the myth of infant determinism   129

9   Let teachers be teachers – not social workers and
    'happiness counsellors'   147

10 Let strangers be friends: how the 'stranger danger' panic
    is creating a hostile adult world   161

    Afterword   179

    Bibliography   181
    Index   197

ACKNOWLEDGEMENTS

I would like to thank in particular Richard Bailey and my agent, Anthony Haynes, for spurring me on to write this book. Special thanks go to Jennie Bristow, my husband Patrick and my sister Karen for reading the first draft of the entire book and giving me detailed and invaluable feedback. Many other people helped me along the way by commenting on draft chapters and providing me with a regular stream of useful material, including: Gerald Allen, Jan Bowman, David Clements, Dolan Cummings, Frank Furedi, Simon Knight, Norman Lewis, Tony Ratner, Jane Sandeman, Stuart Waiton, and my sister Cathinka and sisters-in-law Clare Cox and Trude Guldberg. I am also grateful for the *spiked* team for supporting my decision to take the time out to write the book.

INTRODUCTION

Growing up on the outskirts of Bergen, in Norway, I was given a lot of freedom to roam outside from a very early age. Norwegians have a unique, maybe rather obsessive, love of outdoor pursuits and are therefore a lot more reluctant than in other countries to restrict children's freedom to play outdoors. The local children, my siblings and I were always outdoors, whether in sunshine, rain (all too common in Bergen), sleet or snow, building dens, climbing trees, playing on building sites (against the express instruction of adults), as well as having all kinds of adventures in the woods or by the fjord. As long as we were back for our evening meal we could stay out as long as we wished.

One of the reasons I decided to write this book was that I felt children today were losing out on many childhood experiences that I took for granted. My experience as a primary school teacher and the research for my doctorate in developmental psychology drove home to me how important unsupervised play is for children's social, emotional, cognitive and physical development. Children need to be given space away from adults' watchful eyes – in order to play, experiment, take risks (within a sensible framework provided by adults), test boundaries, have arguments, fight, and learn how to resolve conflicts. This has been my firm belief since I started to study child development;

1

and watching the speed at which that free space is becoming eroded by a culture that prizes 'safety' above all else has weighed upon me as a grave concern.

My worry about modern childhood has also been informed by my position as managing editor of the radical web site *spiked* – a web site that my colleagues and I launched in 2001 with the mission of 'raising the horizons of humanity by waging a culture war of words against misanthropy, priggishness, prejudice, luddism, illiberalism and irrationalism in all their ancient and modern forms'. The dehumanizing impact of a political and cultural world that seeks to lower people's expectations of themselves and those around them was one of our main concerns when launching *spiked*. Adults are increasingly treated as emotionally illiterate beings: parents are constantly talked down to by the government, policymakers and the booming parenting industry, with prescriptive advice about how to parent; teachers are spoonfed about what to teach and given detailed guidance as to how to engage with their pupils; and strangers are treated, not as adults who can play a role in socializing and looking after children but as potential paedophiles.

I noticed that the impact of our safety-obsessed culture, and low expectations of fellow human beings, is particularly stark in relation to children, and was concerned about the impact upon their development. After all, as policymakers are so fond of saying, children are our future – so what kind of future is all this negativity creating?

Since I first started working on *Reclaiming Childhood* a number of books have been published warning that the modern world is damaging our children. Hardly a day has gone by without media exhortations about the harm children are coming to. Apparently just about everything we do is messing up children's lives – whether it be giving them too much, too little, or just the wrong kind of love and attention, feeding them the wrong kind of food or letting them play with the wrong kinds of toys. We are living in a 'junk' world, we are told, and children are suffering as a result.

But the more I looked into all these claims the clearer it became to me that it is not children that are messed up but today's attitude to children. Most of the problems thrown into the pot when discussing childhood today are not, on closer scrutiny, issues about which we should be obsessing.

My aim here is to challenge the dangerous myths about modern childhood and children, and present a more honest, and positive, perspective. Many of the changes we have seen in children's lives over the last centuries and decades are for the good. The key thing that could be holding children back is today's safety-obsessed culture, and low expectations of what they are capable of. By challenging this culture, we can build a better future – and present – for our children and ourselves.

PART I

THE GOOD, THE BAD, AND THE HISTORY

A balance sheet of modern childhood

TWO

COCOONING CHILDREN

Who would envy Huck's battered childhood? Yet he enjoyed something too many children are denied and which adults can provide: opportunities to undertake odysseys of self-discovery outside the goal-driven, overstructured realities of contemporary childhood.

(Stephen Mintz, 2006, p. 384)

The good news is that many of the changes we have seen in children's lives over the past century have made things progressively better for the next generation. Children are healthier and wealthier than ever before; they are given time, attention, protection and education.

The bad news, however, is that society's desire to protect children from the harsh realities of life has in many ways gone too far. There is a real danger that by cocooning children, over-protecting and over-supervising them, society could be denying kids the opportunity to grow up into capable, confident adults.

The Children's Society's 2007 report *The Good Childhood Inquiry* was widely reported as showing that UK children are 'hostages' to parental fears. The UK media ran alarming headlines warning that we are 'rearing children in captivity'. The report argued that parents are today denying children the freedom to mess around with their friends

ONE

A CHILDISH PANIC ABOUT
THE NEXT GENERATION

The relentless forces of modernity are pressing in from all sides, slowly but surely squeezing out the novelty, the independence, the adventure, the wonder, the innocence, the physicality, the solitude – the juice, if you will – from the lives of today's children.

(Chris Mercogliano, 2007, p. ix)

Children are cooped up indoors, passive and apathetic and unable to create their own fun and entertainment. Their imagination is dulled by too many hours of watching television and playing sedentary computer games. They are corrupted by commerce and advertising, tormented by bullies, and traumatized by testing. Or so we are told – over and over and over again.

Exhortations about the harm children are coming to arrive daily via the media, and a plethora of recent books warn about the ill effect modern life is having on the new generation. I would argue that most writers are allowing their rather romanticized view of, and nostalgia for, their own childhoods to influence their inquiry into how children's lives have changed in recent times. Some of their concerns are also shaped by a distinct unease about modern living and a disdain for affluence – even, in some cases, by a snobbish haughtiness towards ignorant, 'materialistic' parents.

In September 2006 the Archbishop of Canterbury and more than 100 eminent experts, including children's authors, scientists, health professionals, teachers and academics joined Sue Palmer, education consultant, broadcaster and author of *Toxic Childhood: How the Modern World is Damaging our Children and What we can Do about It*, in signing a letter to the London *Daily Telegraph* warning that 'modern life leads to more depression among children' (Abbs *et al.* 13 September 2006). Children are suffering, the experts claimed, as a result of our 'junk culture'. The modern world is not providing kids with what they need to develop, which includes: 'real food (as opposed to processed "junk"), real play (as opposed to sedentary, screen-based entertainment), first-hand experience of the world they live in, and regular interaction with the real-life significant adults in their lives' (Abbs *et al.* 13 September 2006).

A year on, the signatories of the original letter were joined by other professionals, academics and writers, claiming that since they first expressed their concern about the marked deterioration in children's mental health 'research evidence supporting this case has continued to mount' (Abbs *et al.* 17 September 2007). In the follow-up letter to the *Daily Telegraph* these experts wrote: 'Compelling examples have included UNICEF's alarming finding that Britain's children are amongst the unhappiest in the developed world, and the children's charity NCH's report of an explosion in children's clinically diagnosable mental health problems' (Abbs *et al.* 17 September 2007).

Apparently children are not only deeply unhappy, they are also stressed out. In October 2007 a report titled *Community Soundings*, published by Cambridge University's Primary Review Group, and hailed as 'the first major investigation into British primary schooling since the Plowden report' of 1967, claimed there is a 'deep anxiety' today about children and childhood. The report's findings generated alarming headlines in the media. 'Pressure of tests "means primary school pupils lose their childhood",' reported the *Times*. 'Study reveals stressed-out 7–11 year-olds,' said the *Guardian*. 'UK youngsters "stressed and depressed",' claimed ITN News.

Writers, commentators and policymakers across the Atlantic have painted an equally bleak picture of modern childhood. In her book *It Takes a Village* then US First Lady Hillary Clinton wrote, 'Everywhere we look, children are under assault: from violence and neglect, from break-up of families, from the temptations of alcohol, sex, and drug abuse, from greed, materialism and spiritual emptiness' (Clinton 1996: 11).

We are told that one worrying outcome of modern living is that children are suffering from something called 'nature deficit disorder'. In his book *Last Child in the Woods* Richard Louv, co-founder and chairman of the US organization Children and Nature Network, argues that children are suffering from 'diminished use of senses, attention difficulties, and higher rates of physical and emotional illnesses' as a result of their 'alienation from nature' (Louv 2005: 34). He argues that modern life is narrowing our senses until our focus is mostly visual, appropriate to the dimensions of a computer monitor or television screen.

Screen-based technologies and expensive toys are reportedly the culprits of all kinds of evil. US child development expert David Elkind writes in *The Power of Play: How Imaginative, Spontaneous Activities Lead to Healthier and Happier Children* that 'Children's play – their inborn disposition for curiosity, imagination and fantasy – is being silenced in the high-tech, commercialised world we have created' (Elkind 2007: ix). The power of play is being destroyed by inexpensive toys available in enormous quantities and seemingly unlimited variety and sedentary screen play, argues Elkind.

Unhappy children, we are told, turn into unhappy, maladjusted and often badly behaved teenagers. According to the UK think-tank IPPR (the Institute for Public Policy Research), British teenagers are 'the worst behaved in Europe'. Research published in the IPPR report *Freedom's Orphans: Raising Youth in a changing World* shows British fifteen-year-olds are more likely to binge-drink, take drugs, have under-age sex and get into fights than their counterparts in Germany, France and Italy (Margo 2006).

A lack of interaction with 'real-life significant adults' in their lives is blamed for teenagers' growing yobbishness. Nick Pearce, director of the IPPR, said:

> Adult role models are vital for children to learn about the norms of behaviour and values in our society, but in Britain children spend less time with their parents than is the case in culturally similar countries ... Because they don't have that structured interaction with adults, it damages their life chances. They are not learning how to behave – how to get on in life – as they need to.
>
> (IPPR 2 November 2006)

Whereas 45 per cent of fifteen-year-old boys in England and 59 per cent of fifteen-year-old boys in Scotland spend most evenings with friends, in France that figure stands at 17 per cent and in Portugal at a mere 7 per cent (Margo 2006).

Childhood has gone 'comprehensively wrong', argues Sue Palmer. Drawing upon the IPPR research, she wrote that we have 'lost track of certain essential and very obvious ingredients for healthy child development ... perhaps most important of all, the opportunity for children to spend time talking to and learning from the loving adults in their lives' (Palmer 27 July 2007). Apparently in a world of limitless affluence and labour-saving devices we come to expect everything to be available at the flick of a switch, and therefore don't realize that child rearing is not conducive to quick-fix solutions. Today's parents care more about 'stuff than relationships', complains Palmer: 'Earning enough for a new kitchen matters more than chatting to the children in the old one' (Palmer 27 July 2007).

Around the same time, a report by the UK Children's Society, entitled *The Good Childhood Inquiry*, was widely reported as showing that UK children are 'hostages' to parental fears, by being denied the freedom to mess around outside with their friends. Parents cannot win. On one hand, they are reportedly allowing teenagers to spend too much time hanging around with their friends outside, not spending 'quality time' with their children. On the other, they are creating a generation of 'battery children' who are cooped up inside and denied the freedom to socialize.

The one thing everyone seems to agree on is that growing up in modern times – particularly in Britain and America – is Really Bad. And the much publicized UNICEF report *Child Poverty in Perspective: An Overview of Child Well-being in Rich Countries* apparently proves the doom-mongers right (UNICEF 2007). As is repeated *ad nauseam* in the press, the UK ranked bottom and the US second from the bottom in UNICEF's league table of twenty-one industrialized countries for child well-being. Children's Society chief executive Bob Reitemeier said, 'We simply cannot ignore these shocking findings. UNICEF's report is a wake-up call to the fact that, despite being a rich country, the UK is failing children and young people in a number of crucial ways' (BBC Online 14 February 2007). Al Aynsley Green, the Children's Commissioner for England, was equally emphatic, if a little more obscure: 'There is a crisis at the heart of our society and we must not continue to ignore the impact of our attitudes towards children and young people and the effect that this has on their wellbeing' (Johnston 15 February 2007).

In the US children's advocates welcomed the UNICEF report. Linda Spears, Vice-president of Corporate Communications and Development at the Child Welfare League of America (CWLA) said, 'I'm more optimistic now than I've ever been that this may help galvanize energy on Capitol Hill and encourage advocates to pay attention' (Johnson 20 February 2007).

In the round, it seems it is pretty awful to be a child in the UK and the US today. But how seriously should we take this panicked discussion about the state of childhood?

Reasons to be cheerful

Most of the problems thrown into the pot when discussing con-temporary childhood are not, on closer scrutiny, issues we should be obsessing about. The argument in *Reclaiming Childhood* is that this depressing depiction of modern childhood is not just flawed and inaccu-rate but potentially damaging to both children and adults. It could be a

11

self-fulfilling prophecy should some children (though by no means all of them) become depressed, anxious, isolated and stressed. The constant panicking about children's wellbeing by governments, the media and advocacy groups does children no good. Nor is it good for parents. As sociologist Frank Furedi shows in *Paranoid Parenting*, it is likely to make parents fret even more about their children and increase the insecurities and hang-ups they have about their abilities as parents (Furedi 2001).

Journalist Libby Brooks provides a rather fitting description of society's gloomy view of children's lives in *The Story of Childhood: Growing up in Modern Britain* (Brooks 2006). 'Over the past three decades, worries about children's well-being have been amplified to an excruciating pitch,' she writes. 'Childhood has become the crucible into which is ground each and every adult anxiety – about sex, consumerism, technology, safety, achievement, respect, the proper shape of life. This is a time of child-panic' (Brooks 2006: 16).

For centuries people have argued that the younger generation is more alienated and worse behaved than previously. In *Huck's Raft: A History of American Childhood* Steven Mintz notes, 'Ever since the Pilgrims departed from Plymouth in 1620, fearful that "their posterity would be in danger to degenerate and be corrupted" in the Old World, Americans have experienced repeated panics over the younger generation' (Mintz 2006: ix). Child-panic is clearly not a completely new phenomenon, but today it has indeed reached an 'excruciating pitch'.

It is time to take a more critical look at today's doom-mongering about children. Interpretations of social, economic and lifestyle changes, and their effect on children's lives, are easily clouded by the researchers' own experiences, outlooks and feelings. Rather than pointing the finger at easy 'junk' targets and labelling children as fragile and easily damaged, we need to try to identify what the real problems are – and how much they matter.

UNICEF's league table on child well-being

Let's start by taking a closer look at what the UNICEF report – the so-called 'proof' that modern childhood is in dire straights – actually tells us. The report claims to measure and compare, for the first time, overall child well-being across six dimensions. These include material well-being, health and safety, education, peer and family relation-ships, behaviours and risks, as well as young people's own subjective sense of their own well-being. In total, forty separate indicators of child well-being – from relative poverty and child safety to educa-tional achievement and drug abuse – were brought together to present a picture of the lives of children.

Material well-being was measured on the basis of three separate components: relative income poverty (that is, the percentage of chil-dren living in homes with incomes below 50 per cent of the national median), the number of households without jobs, and children's own reported level of deprivation. But what do any of the measures really tell us? A household without jobs in the UK is going to have a higher standard of living than a household without jobs in Hungary or Portugal, for instance. Also, as the UNICEF report acknowledges, there is a big difference between relative and absolute poverty:

> [The report] shows, for example, that the child poverty rate in the United States is higher than in Hungary, but fails to show that 50 per cent of median income (for a couple with two children) is approximately $7,000 in Hungary and $24,000 in the United States.
> (UNICEF 2007: 6)

When it comes to education the UK ranks among the top ten coun-tries in the OECD's Programme of International Student Assessment (PISA). PISA involves giving 250,000 students in forty-one countries a two-hour examination designed to measure their abilities in reading, maths and science. Finland, Canada, Australia, and Japan are top of the table, with Greece, Italy, Spain and Portugal in the bottom four places. Norway and Denmark, often hailed for their education sys-tems, are found in the eighteenth and nineteenth places respectively – a long way behind the UK. Britain's education system is far from perfect: but these findings should warn us against the assumption that it is that much worse than the education systems of other countries.

13

The UK also has its highest rankings on some of the more objective measures, such as health and safety. Here countries were assessed according to several components: birth weight, infant mortality rates, immunization rates, and deaths and injuries from accidents. After Sweden, the UK has the second lowest rate of deaths from accidents and injuries for young people under nineteen years of age. The US has the second highest, after New Zealand. However, compared with non-OECD countries such as Latvia, Russia or Israel, child accidental death rates are relatively low in the UK and US.

Contrary to the claims made repeatedly by media reports, the UNICEF report did not conclusively reveal that the UK and US are the worst countries in the Western world to grow up in. In fact, it didn't contain many conclusive insights at all. It did bring together lots of interesting material that compared and contrasted children's different experiences in different countries, but the data can be interpreted in various different ways.

Wayward youth

The 2006 IPPR report *Freedom's Orphans: Raising Youth in a Changing World* was again accepted unquestioningly by the media as evidence that things are Really Bad in the UK. Several papers ran with the headline 'UK youths "among worst in Europe".' According to BBC Online, 'Measured against German, French and Italian youngsters, British 15-year-olds are drunk more often and involved in more fights, and a higher proportion have had sex' (BBC Online 2 November 2006).

Nick Pearce, director of the IPPR, said that UK youth are 'disconnected' from the adults around them. They lack the 'soft social skills' displayed by teens in Europe who spend more time in the company of adults: 'Because they don't have that structured interaction with adults, it damages their life chances' (BBC Online 2 November 2006). But what evidence is there that UK youth do not have 'structured interaction with adults'?

One of the findings from *Freedom's Orphans* that was highlighted by the media was that 'British teenagers spend more time with other teenagers than in other countries' (IPPR 26 July 2007). Not only is it unquestioningly assumed that teenagers hanging out together is a worrying phenomenon, but the report does not in fact show that UK youth spend more time with their peers than all other European youth.

Freedom's Orphans actually found that the proportion of fifteen-year-olds spending time with their friends 'four or more evenings a week' was higher in England than in *some* other countries – such as Poland, Portugal and Denmark, among others. In England 45 per cent of boys and 34 per cent of girls reportedly hang out together most evenings. In Italy the figures stand at 25 per cent for boys and 14 per cent for girls. But there were also several countries – notably Ukraine, Finland and, a country often hailed as a haven of social cohesion, Norway – where a *higher* percentage of youngsters than in England were found to spend most evenings with their friends. In Norway approximately half of both boys and girls claimed to spend four or more evenings a week with their friends.

The IPPR report opens with the gloomy pronouncement that 'Commentators fear that British youth are on the verge of mental breakdown, at risk from antisocial behaviour, self-harm, drug and alcohol abuse' and concludes that 'These concerns are, to an extent, borne out in IPPR's findings and other research, presented in this report' (Margo 2006: vii). But are these concerns borne out in reality? It is often assumed that 'peer pressure' – particularly among teenagers – is a bad thing. But, as I argue in Chapter 5, friendships serve an important social function, both in early childhood and in adolescence. Why should we assume that if youngsters hang out with each other outside school hours they are necessarily disaffected from adult society?

When looking at the data gathered by the IPPR, it is unclear on what basis everybody has drawn such negative conclusions. The IPPR found that 'the proportion of young people whose parents spend time "just talking" to them several times a week' was 62 per cent in the UK. Granted, this figure is slightly lower than some countries, including Denmark at 69 per cent and Hungary at 89 per cent. But the UK figure is higher than a number of other countries', including Spain at 59 per cent and Germany at 41 per cent. The proportion of young people whose parents 'eat a main meal with them around a table several times a week' was 64 per cent in the UK, quite a lot lower than the 93 per cent in Italy. But we need to bear in mind that there will be cultural factors at play here. The main meal of the day has historically featured more centrally in the lives of families in southern European countries than in northern European countries. Yet, even in the UK, the IPPR figures show that the majority of adults reportedly eat a main meal with their children most evenings.

While the negative presentation of childhood popularized by studies like these tends to dominate the general perception of British kids in crisis, it is important to note that not all studies, or critics, endorse this downbeat view. The Future Foundation report *The Changing Face of Parenting* completely contradicts the claims that parents are too busy making money to give their children enough time and attention, arguing instead:

> Over the last few decades the proportion of women participating in the workforce has grown significantly ... While this may lead people to think that the amount of time parents tend to spend on childcare has decreased, in fact, the reality is just the opposite.
>
> (Future Foundation 2006: 6)

Today's parents are spending an average of ninety-nine minutes a day engaged in child care, which is far more than the twenty-five minutes a day spent by parents in 1975. This is in stark contrast to the public and policy perception. The Future Foundation found that in just three years 'the proportion of people who feel that parents spend less time with their children than they used to has grown by ten per cent to an overwhelming 80 per cent' (Future Foundation 2006: 12). The worry about parents' time deficit seems to be based far more on a generalized sense of anxiety and guilt about what parents are putting into family life than on actual facts and measurable minutes.

In November 2007 a group of twelve Year 9 pupils from a comprehensive school in Muswell Hill, north London, wrote and edited an issue of the *Times* (London) supplement, *times2*. Introducing the supplement, *times2* editor, Sandra Parson, wrote:

> What are teenagers like? We think we know, and certainly read enough lurid stories about them. They are binge-drinking bullying yobs. They are neurotic wrecks driven to breakdown because of pressure of exams ... They spend their time watching reality TV, or in unsuitable internet chatrooms where they are prime fodder for perverts.
>
> (Parson 26 November 2007)

But the pupils from Fortismere comprehensive were nothing like their popular image. Writing about their passions, fears and pastimes it emerged that they 'worry about gangs but they aren't bullied' and, as Parsons writes, 'are far too savvy on the internet to be tricked': 'They used to like reality TV but now find it boring. They like YouTube and MySpace but not Bebo and Facebook ... Most of all they would like parents to stop being so overprotective – and to trust them' (Parson 26 November 2007).

Generation anxiety

In her book *The Price of Privilege: How Parental Pressure and Material Advantage are Creating a Generation of Disconnected and Unhappy Kids* clinical psychologist Madeline Levine tells us that the US is facing an epidemic of depression, anxiety and substance abuse among children and young people (Levine 2006). And this is happening not only among the disadvantaged but in affluent families, too.

Her claims seem to be backed up by a number of reports. The World Health Organization (WHO) 2001 report entitled *Mental Health: New Understanding, New Hope* claims that between 10 per cent and 20 per cent of young people suffer from mental health or behavioural disorders. According to the report, mental disorders can be 'diagnosed as reliably and accurately as most of the common physical disorders' (WHO 2001: 22). Hans Troedsson, WHO director for child and adolescent health, later warned: 'The international health community is concerned about the mental health status of our young. It is a time-bomb that is ticking and without the right action now millions of our children growing up will feel the effects' (WHO 2005: 83).

Similarly, research commissioned by the UK Department of Health in 2003 apparently shows that serious mental health problems are far more common among young people than previously recognized. A survey of more than 1,000 fifteen to twenty-one-year-olds found that most young people know someone who has self-harmed, had depression or suffered an eating disorder. Even more worryingly, a third of young people 'know someone who has attempted suicide' (BBC Online 10 February 2003). The findings coincided with the launch of Read the Signs, a government initiative aiming to encourage young people to understand and discuss mental health issues through a dedicated web site and virtual games.

Carol Midgley, journalist for the *Times* (London) wrote in a feature article, 'We are being told continually that the incidence of childhood depression is increasing. Between 1991 and 2001 the number of children prescribed antidepressants in the UK rose by 70 per cent, amid an apparent epidemic of self-harm and eating disorders' (Midgley 26 June 2007). Indeed, these are frightening figures. But, looking beyond the press releases to life as it is lived by young people, I wonder how we can possibly be in the grip of an epidemic of misery and self-abuse on the scale implied by the reports and campaigns.

My nephew, who started at a state secondary school in London a couple of years ago, does not recognize these bleak descriptions of modern childhood. He thinks most of the kids in his year are happy enough – and far from the miserable little creatures they are often described as. He remembers a couple of children from his primary school looking sad and dejected a lot of the time. Their unhappiness and despondency stood out because they were so unlike the other kids, whose emotions would yo-yo from ecstatic happiness to woeful misery (often over the most trivial matter), but who in most part were perfectly contented little creatures.

Similarly when I asked a group of US students – who, after all, are among the wealthiest and most privileged in the world, and, by most accounts, therefore the unhappiest – what they thought of these claims, they all looked perplexed. They thought that on the whole they had happy childhoods. 'But if they're talking about adolescence,' one student piped up, 'I might agree. Surely it's the most distressing time of everyone's life?'

Speaking for myself, the teenage years formed a miserable and meaningless time, and I would not relive those years for anything. I have long assumed that misery and introspection are what being a teenager is about; and 'teenage angst' is not a pet theme of adolescent novels and magazines for nothing. Of course, some people are perfectly contented throughout their adolescence, and maybe all those who are berating today's youth for their aimlessness and bad behaviour never lost their footing during their teenage years. Or maybe they have just conveniently forgotten what they were like when they were young. But it is far from obvious to me that today's youth are any more miserable or badly behaved than my generation were; and when studies set out to quantify the depths of this misery and the extent to which it has grown we should hardly be surprised if they find what they are looking for.

What is true is that many more children and young people are on anti-depressants and other forms of medication today, particularly in the US but also in Britain and other parts of Europe. Figures published by the UK Department for Children, Schools and Families (DCSF), formerly the Department for Education and Skills (DfES), in July 2007 show a huge year-on-year increase over the past decade in drugs prescribed by British general practitioners for behavioural and mental disorders in children and young people (BBC Online 23 July 2007). And apparently there is a demand for yet more drugs. The British Medical Association (BMA) report *Child and Adolescent Mental Health* also claims that 'at any one time in the UK, one in ten children under sixteen years of age has a clinically diagnosed mental health disorder' (BMA 2006: 2). Emotional disorders, in particular anxieties, but also phobias and depression, are the most common mental health problems in children, the report claims.

The children's charity NCH brought out a briefing in 2007, quoted extensively in the press, claiming that the prevalence of emotional problems and conduct disorders has doubled since the 1990s, to the current figure of one in ten children.

Again, however, these figures should be interpreted with care. According to Professor Sue Bailey, chair of the Child and Adolescent Faculty at the Royal College of Psychiatrists in London, the 'one in ten' figure highlighted by the NCH is not new. There is little evidence that incidences of childhood depression are rising: 'In fact, [Department for Health figures] show that the prevalence of mental disorders among five to sixteen-year-olds in 2004 have remained broadly unchanged from the previous survey in 1999' (BBC Online 20 June 2007). Also, the one in ten figure, Bailey claims, covers a wide range of problems – from the relatively minor to the very serious.

Professor David Healy, a consultant psychiatrist at Cardiff University College of Medicine, believes the number of children with severe mental health problems – those who need treatment – is nearer one in 100 than one in ten. He argues that the higher figure can be explained by doctors stretching the label of depression to cover an ever wider range of unhappiness. Healy has not been shy in taking the psychiatric profession to task for being 'seduced' by the drug industry. Reports about childhood depression in prestigious scientific journals are no more trustworthy than marketing infomercials, he claims. In other words, the current demand for drugs has been manufactured (Healy 2004, 2005).

In addition to this, says Healy, parents are today less willing to tolerate variations in how their children behave, often overreacting to peculiar behaviours and mood swings. A similar point is made by Sami Timimi, consultant child and adolescent psychiatrist: '[M]ore childhood behaviours previously considered normal are now seen as problematic, and problematic behaviours are more likely to be medicalised … The increase in rates of childhood depression in Western society may reflect a lowering of the threshold for the diagnosis' (Timimi 2004: 1394).

It is not only the medical profession that is sceptical about how 'real' the rise in childhood disorders actually is. Among parents of school-age children the idea that children are increasingly being 'statemented' as having special needs, in order to give them educational advantages, or put on medication or therapy because they are occasionally noisy or naughty, has become a standard feature of school-gates discussion.

The fascinating book *Shyness: How Normal Behaviour became a Sickness*, by the Chicago-based research professor Christopher Lane, shows how everyday emotions have become increasingly medicalized. 'In my mother's generation, shy people were seen as introverted and perhaps a bit awkward, but never mentally ill,' he writes. 'Adults admired their bashfulness, associated it with bookishness, reserve, and a yen for solitude. But shyness isn't just shyness any more. It is a disease. It has a variety of overwrought names, including "social anxiety" and "avoidant personality disorder", afflictions said to trouble millions' (Lane 2007: 1). Shyness now allegedly almost rivals depression in magnitude, a 'sickness' for which 'almost 200 million prescriptions are filled every year' in the US (Lane 2007: 5).

Lane has taken shyness as a test case to show how society is being over-diagnosed and over-medicated. He has charted, in intricate detail, the route by which the psychiatric profession came to give credence to the labelling of everyday emotions as 'disorders' – a situation that has resulted in more and more people being deemed to be mentally ill. His painstaking research shows how the *Diagnostic and Statistical Manual of Mental Disorders (DSM)*, the Bible of the psychiatric profession worldwide, has been transformed, by a handful of psychiatrists, from the thin handbook it was until the 1980s into the hefty tome it is today, with hundreds of new, poorly specified and poorly researched syndromes being added. Lane explains:

> Beginning in 1980, with much fanfare and confidence in its revised diagnoses, the American Psychiatric Association added 'social phobia', 'avoidant personality disorder', and several similar conditions to the third edition of its massively expanded Diagnostic and Statistical Manual of Mental Disorders. In this 500-page volume ... the introverted individual morphed into the mildly

psychotic person whose symptoms included being aloof, being dull, and simply 'being alone'.

(Lane 2007: 2–3)

It took a roomful of psychiatrists only a few years to massively expand their manual and turn routine emotions into medical conditions, Lane shows. The fourth edition of *DSM* appeared in 1994 with 400 more pages than previously, and dozens of new disorders. WHO's claim that mental disorders can be 'diagnosed as reliably and accurately as most of the common physical disorders' is clearly laughable; instead it seems that mental disorders can be created on a whim and attributed to all sorts of actually quite normal people.

It is also worth pointing out that whatever figures we do accept – whether it be one in ten or one in a hundred – the vast majority of children are *not* depressed and, on the whole, are coping rather well with the apparent tsunami of stresses and worries brought about by modern living.

The myth of stressed schoolkids

In response to the publication of the Primary Review in October 2007 an article in the UK *Independent* claimed, 'Our young children are anxious, badly behaved, stressed, depressed and obsessed with the cult of celebrity, according to the first in-depth report into primary schooling for four decades' (Garner 12 October 2007). The *Daily Mail* painted an equally scary picture: 'Family breakdown, exam pressure, celebrity culture and crime … all are robbing children of their innocence' (Clark 11 October 2007).

In truth, the study did not show that children are 'stressed out' or 'depressed'. It did not investigate family breakdown, the prevalence of crime, or any other objective measure of the quality of modern childhood, for that matter. All that *Community Soundings* investigated was the views of 757 subjects in eighty-seven 'witness sessions' – commonly known as focus groups, a method well known to be limited in reliably surveying people's opinions – in different parts of England.

The participants included community representatives, employers, religious leaders, parents, governors, head teachers, teachers, teaching assistants and children.

Robin Alexander, who oversaw the research of *Community Soundings*, said, 'What struck us was that the overall message everywhere was the same. People are very worried about childhood' (Frean 12 October 2007). The report stated:

> We were frequently told children are under intense and perhaps excessive pressure from the policy-driven demands of their schools and the commercially driven values of the wider society; that family life and community are breaking down; that there is a pervasive loss of respect and empathy both within and between generations; that life outside the school gates is increasingly insecure and dangerous ... Parents felt that they had to keep their children under close supervision in order to secure their safety, yet were unhappy that this was necessary ... They were nostalgic for the childhood freedoms they themselves had enjoyed.
>
> (Primary Review 2007: 1)

Given that *Community Soundings* was based on witness sessions – that is, on the views and feelings of fairly small focus groups – might the respondents have been influenced by something other than hard facts and evidence about childhood? It's worth noting that the witness sessions took place early in 2007, following months of daily warnings about how modern life is damaging kids. Indeed, it was in the middle of the data-gathering process – February 2007 – that UNICEF published its 'bad news' report on child well-being.

Bombarded by a daily diet of headlines about British children being too fat, too inactive, and under threat from criminals, bullies and strangers, and claims that Britain is lagging behind the rest of the developed world in the well-being stakes, it is not surprising that a survey of opinion found people expressing concern about kids being stressed and depressed.

Good-news stories about children's lives are often subsumed by a titillating focus on the alleged dangers facing our kids. Some aspects of the *Community Soundings* report could be interpreted positively. For example, it is encouraging that 'children were by far the most optimistic of our witnesses', suggesting that young people have a more positive view of their lives than the adults who panic and fret about them (Primary Review 2007: 20). Alas, this sentence was buried in the report – neither the Cambridge Primary Review Group's overview of the report, nor the press release that accompanied it, drew attention to the finding about young people's relative optimism.

Instead the overview stressed that the outlook of the participants as a whole was pervaded by a sense of deep pessimism about the future, and said that children themselves were not immune to such an outlook. It is true that children are not immune to society's rising sense of doom and gloom; for example, a survey conducted by the supermarket chain Somerfield earlier in 2007 found that many school-age British children have sleepless nights or nightmares about climate catastrophe.

It would be wrong, however, to assume that children unquestioningly internalize the miserabilist culture of contemporary society. Media reports claimed that *Community Soundings* found that children are 'stressed out' about exams. In fact the report found that 'the children were more ambivalent about SATs than any other constituency'. Some of the young respondents did describe SATs as 'scary', and said that sitting exams 'puts them under pressure'. But they could also see the positive side of testing: 'Tests tell teachers, and us, how we are doing' (Primary Review 2007: 15). Nothing in the children's responses suggested they were seriously 'stressed out' about exams. Instead it was the teachers who were surveyed for the report who described SATs as 'highly stressful' and claimed that they 'put children and teachers under intolerable pressure' (Primary Review 2007: 19).

For me, the main lesson of *Community Soundings*, which is the first in a series of thirty-two reports that has been published by Cambridge University's Primary Review, is the urgent need to counter today's doom-mongering about children's lives. We need to recognize that 'modern living' is not the problem: whether it be affluence, new technologies, greater mobility or academic pressure, none of these is a problem in and of itself. The problem lies with adult society, and the extent to which the culture of fear that dominates today's society is holding children back. Adults should stop projecting their fears and uncertainties on to children, labelling them with the 'stressed' and 'depressed' tag, and instead allow children to grow and flourish with a balance of sensible adult guidance and some youthful independence.

Fat and fiction

For much of the twenty-first century we have been subjected to daily warnings from campaigners, scientists and government spokespeople about the health effects of the 'escalating rates' of childhood obesity. 'The fat child has become a new kind of folk devil, a rapacious, insufficiently socialised monster', David Buckingham, Director of the Centre for the Study of Children, Youth and Media, astutely points out (Buckingham 2005: 5).

Warnings from the House of Commons Health Select Committee in 2004 were particularly stark:

> Should the gloomier scenarios relating to obesity turn out to be true, the sight of amputees will become much more familiar in the streets of Britain. There will be many more blind people. There will be a huge demand for kidney dialysis … Indeed, this will be the first generation where children die before their parents as a consequence of childhood obesity.
>
> (Health Committee 26 May 2004)

This claim that 'children will die before their parents' has popped up again and again in the media. It is assumed, without question, that children are unhealthier today than at any time in living memory. 'The people of the developed world have suddenly noticed we've been poisoning our children,' writes Sue Palmer in *Toxic Childhood*. 'The food we've let them eat over the last decade or so – ever richer in sugar, salt, additives and the wrong sort of fat – now contains very little nourishment. Instead of building healthy bodies, it's simply making children fatter and unhealthier by the year' (Palmer 2007: 21). Scientists and policymakers are falling over themselves to accentuate the scale of the problem – with constant references to obesity being 'as bad as climate change' – or worse. It is 'a time bomb waiting to go off', we are told.

UK Health Secretary Alan Johnson has warned that 'We cannot afford not to act. We are facing a potential crisis on the scale of climate change and it is in everybody's interest to turn things round' (Reuters 14 October 2007). The US Surgeon General managed to outdo the British alarmists, claiming that obesity is a greater threat than weapons of mass destruction.

In October 2007 Prime Minister Gordon Brown earmarked funding for 'a long-term action plan to fight obesity' after the government-commissioned Foresight report claimed that, by 2050, '60 per cent of adult men, 50 per cent of adult women and about 25 per cent of all children under sixteen could be obese' (Foresight 2007: 2). The report warned that 'human biology is being overwhelmed by the effects of today's "obesogenic" environment, with its abundance of energy dense food, motorised transport and sedentary lifestyles' (Foresight 2007: 2).

Such claims have been so often made in the ongoing panic about childhood obesity that it would be easy just to nod along. But we should interrogate these scary statistics, and the presumptions behind them.

For some critics, the worrying 'epidemic' of childhood obesity is less about the size of children than it is about the growing weight of articles, studies and policy documents that have turned this into a panic. As Patrick Basham and John Luik, at the Washington-based Democracy Institute and authors of *Diet Nation*, argue:

> The media has picked up on the [obesity] scares and turned them into a kind of orthodoxy. For instance, the term 'childhood obesity' occurred only twice in the *Guardian* in 1999. In 2004 it occurred 201 times, almost four times a week. The public have become convinced that the 'epidemic' is a fact.
>
> (Basham and Luik 27 November 2006)

It is true that Body Mass Index (a figure consisting of height squared divided by weight squared) statistics show a significant increase in overweight adults over the past decade. But, as Basham points out in an interview with the UK *Independent*, 'This is an extraordinary case of moving the methodological goalposts: in 1997, the BMI classification of being overweight was changed from 27 to 25. At a stroke, millions of people previously classed as normal suddenly became overweight, with no good reason to explain the change' (Feinmann 23 October 2007).

The British Social Issues Research Centre (SIRC) has also taken the time to analyse the government obesity statistics, concluding that the 'widespread assumptions about "exponential" rises in obesity and the "epidemic" scale of the problem were not justified' (Marsh 22 May 2005). The government report *Health Survey for England 2003* shows that the average weight of boys under sixteen years of age in fact fell – albeit very slightly – from 32 kg in 1995 to 31.9 kg in 2003 (National Centre for Social Research 2004). For girls of the same age the average weight rose from 32 kg in 1995 to 32.4 kg in 2003. In the same period the BMI of boys rose by 0.6 from 17.6 to 18.2, and the BMI of girls rose by 0.5 from 18.0 to 18.5. Not exactly epidemic proportions, are they?

The scale of obesity among children has been wildly exaggerated. So too have the health consequences of having excess body weight. The claim that being 'overweight' or 'modestly obese' leads to a higher risk of premature death is not supported by research. A large-scale study by the US Centers for Disease Control and Prevention shows that being underweight (having a BMI under 18.5) or having a BMI of more than 35 (bearing in mind a person with a BMI of 30 or over is classed as 'obese') is associated with increased mortality (Flegal *et al.* 2005). The mortality rates for 'overweight' people (those with a BMI between 25 and 30) were actually lower than for those people of 'normal' weight. 'These findings are consistent with the increases in life expectancy in the United States and the declining mortality rates from ischemic heart disease,' the researchers concluded (Flegal *et al.* 2005: 1865).

Rather than children 'dying before their parents', evidence indicates that life expectancy is rising and will continue to rise – in great part due to vast improvements in most children's diets over the past hundreds of years.

When comparing children's diets today with, say, the nineteenth century, the idea that we are 'poisoning our children' with 'junk food' can be seen only as ridiculous. Children today have a far more varied and healthy diet than at any time in history. There are a number of fruits and vegetables that today's children regularly eat that I hadn't even heard of as a child growing up in Norway. A daily supply of fruit and vegetables (apart from potatoes, which were a staple part of every meal) were considered a luxury for Norwegian children in the 1970s. If we go further back, to the eighteenth and nineteenth centuries, the main concern of parents was not whether their children were eating enough fruit 'n' veg but to be able to fill their children's bellies with anything roughly edible, in order to stave off their almost constant hunger.

Karl Marx provides a vivid description in *Capital* of 'the incredible adulteration' of bread – the staple part of children's limited diet in those days. The report by the House of Commons committee on 'The adulteration of articles of food (1855–56)', Marx recounts:

> roused not the heart of the public but its stomach. Englishmen, always well up on the Bible, knew well enough that man ... is commanded to eat his bread in the sweat of his brow, but they did not know that he had to eat daily in his bread a certain quantity of human perspiration mixed with the discharge of abscesses, cobwebs, dead black-beetles, and putrid German yeast, without counting alum, sand, and other agreeable mineral ingredients.
> (Marx 1983: 238)

Things were not much better for many children by the early 1900s. Esther Peel, born in a Northamptonshire village, was the daughter of a pit labourer. Her three younger brothers all died of malnutrition as infants. 'I used to have to stay at home to mind the baby,' she recounts in the book of the BBC series *A Labour of Love: The Experience of Parenthood in Britain, 1900–1950*. 'My mother used to say, "There's a cup of sop in the oven for the baby." All it consisted of was bread, water and a sparkle of sugar ... I was hungry too so I used to have a spoonful of it' (Humphries and Gordon 1993: 128). For their main meal of the day Esther and her older brother used to get a slice of bread 'dipped in this horrible fat'. 'I was always hungry,' adds Peel. 'We were poverty-stricken. Really, my baby brothers starved to death. They just faded' (Humphries and Gordon 1993: 129). If we were to label anything 'junk food' surely it would be the diets of previous generations?

In 2007 the Office for Communications (OfCom) enacted its ban on television advertising of 'junk food' to children. Foods are junk – or unhealthy – according to a nutrient profiling model constructed by the UK Food Standards Agency (FSA) if they are high in fat, salt or sugar.

Yet Vincent Marks, co-editor *of Panic Nation: Unpicking the Myths we're Told about Food and Health*, argues that there is no such thing as junk food. 'Junk food is an oxymoron,' he told BBC Online:

> Food is either good – that is, it is enjoyable to eat and will sustain life – or it is good food that has gone bad, meaning that it has deteriorated and gone off. To label a food as 'junk' is just another way of saying, 'I disapprove of it.'
>
> (O'Neill 3 October 2005)

Also, as Emily Hill has pointed out on *spiked*, the FSA's nutritional profiling model 'will mean that foods such as cheese, raisins and bran flakes – as well as breast milk, if it were available in shops – will be branded "unhealthy" and thus banned from kids' (Hill 9 February 2007).

Additives, E-numbers and other chemicals

'A plausible connection to tantrums, poor concentration and slow progress at school is understood to have been found in a study to be published by the government's Food Standards Agency'. So warned the *Daily Mail* in September 2007, while a *Guardian* headline claimed: 'After thirty years of debate, fears over children's food confirmed.' But what evidence is there that food and drink additives make children behave badly?

The study, commissioned by the Food Standards Agency (FSA), was carried out by a team at Southampton University. Investigating the effect of different mixtures of additives – based on artificial colours and benzoate preservative – on the behaviour of a random sample of 300 children, the researchers found an effect of *certain* mixtures of additives on *some* children. Dr Andrew Wadge, the FSA's chief scientist, said: 'We have revised our advice to consumers: if a child shows signs of hyperactivity or ADHD then eliminating the colours used in the ... study from their diet might have some beneficial effects' (FSA 11 September 2007). However, as Nigel Hawkes, health editor of the *Times* (London), pointed out, 'The size of the effect, roughly, was an increase in hyperactivity that represented less than a tenth of that seen in children diagnosed with ADHD (attention deficit hyperactivity disorder)' (Hawkes 6 September 2007).

Many have leapt to the conclusion from this study, and others showing similarly small effects of food additives on the behaviour of children with ADHD, that artificial additives are bad for children and should be avoided at all costs. Such conclusions are assumed to support the time-honoured 'commonsense' prejudice that additives make children hyperactive: and the difference between this idea and the specific research findings goes unremarked. So the social networking site Netmums warns:

> About 400 E-number additives and several thousand unnamed flavours are used in the food we eat. On average we each eat about 4 kg of food additives each year. That means that your child may have eaten its own body weight of additives by the time he or she is an adult!

Parents are encouraged to start reading food and drink labels to avoid E-numbers. This may seem like the sensible, responsible thing to do –

unless you consider that it is a pretty misleading exercise for parents. As dietician Ursula Arens has explained, E-numbers merely 'communicate that [the food additive] has been approved for its intended use across the EU' (Arens 28 January 2006). Many E-numbers are found naturally in foods and may include essential vitamins, such as ascorbic acid (vitamin C, E300) and tocopherols (vitamin E, E306–9).

In response to all the fretting about additives, E-numbers and chemicals, Andrew Cockburn, Director of Toxico-Logical Consulting, points out that in the UK in 1840 the average life expectancy was only forty years of age; today it is nearer to eighty. 'That makes us the healthiest hypochondriacs that ever existed,' he says (Cockburn 2006). In the late nineteenth century the population was indeed exposed to a number of hazardous chemicals. In 1871 the Royal Sanitary Commission noted that the water in the Bradford Canal was so contaminated that a dropped lamp could set it alight. Chemicals used in hat making gave off mercury vapour, causing muscle tremors, distorted vision and slurred speech. Hence the origin of the phrase 'mad as a hatter'. This chemical, and many more, are now carefully regulated, allowing us to live better and healthier lives.

But that does not stop some people from fretting. Not many of them end up as red-faced as the Californian city councillors who in 2004 took steps to protect the public from the 'potentially deadly' chemical dihydrogen monoxide. A hoax web site had warned that this 'odourless, tasteless chemical' kills thousands of people every year, mainly through accidental inhalation. The web site pointed out that dihydrogen monoxide causes severe burns in its gaseous state and severe tissue damage through prolonged exposure in its solid state. City officials considered banning foam cups after they learned the chemical was used in their production. But dihydrogen monoxide is, of course, H_2O; in other words, water.

outdoors – a freedom that they themselves once enjoyed and cherished. Back in 2001 the Children's Society and the Children's Play Council likewise warned that children are being prevented from playing in their own neighbourhoods. Cars, bullying and parents' fears about strangers are turning them not so much into couch potatoes as couch prisoners, claimed Ian Sparks, then chief executive of the Children's Society.

In *Detoxing Childhood*, her how-to sequel to the grim *Toxic Childhood*, Sue Palmer claims that we are raising a generation of 'battery' children. 'This is the first time in human history that children *en masse* have been reared in captivity.' she wrote (Palmer 2007: 51). And US educationalist Chris Mercogliano, in his book *In Defense of Childhood: Protecting Kids' Inner Wilderness*, points to the 'supreme irony' that, while we have eliminated many risks from children's lives, 'the perceived danger is causing us to fence them in as never before' (Mercogliano 2007: 3). He describes how childhood from the middle of the twentieth century has increasingly been viewed as an accident waiting to happen:

> The public service announcement 'Do you know where your children are?' was intoned like a mantra between evening TV programs, and as the twentieth century moved fearfully to a close, the parental imperative to keep kids close to home, confined to playgrounds and playrooms, had become nearly universal.
>
> (Mercogliano 2007: 2)

The hyperbolic way in which the contemporary trend towards cocooning children is sometimes discussed reached its zenith in a *Guardian* headline in September 2004. 'Bred in captivity: for the first time in 4 million years of human history, we are effectively trapping children indoors,' the newspaper warned (Gill 20 September 2004). The idea that we have had 4 million years of human history will be news to most palaeontologists, while the notion that children have always and for ever had the time and space to play outdoors rather than, say, work long and brutal hours in factories will be news to most historians.

Much of the discussion about 'battery children' overstates the problem. In seeking to pin the blame on individual parents' anxieties, those who decry the decline of outdoor play are often naive and unfair. It is true that children's freedom to play and roam outdoors has been restricted in recent years, and that this has negative consequences for their development. But the cause of this shift indoors is a broader cultural obsession with risk, which has had a major impact upon policymakers, public institutions, and media debate, as well as upon parents. In challenging this culture, it is important to be clear about what the problems are, and resist pat explanations of their cause.

The growing concern about children being 'raised in captivity' often goes hand in hand with misgivings about the younger generation's lack of access to the natural environment. US journalist and writer Richard Louv argues in *Last Child in the Woods: Saving our Children from Nature-Deficit Disorder* that children are suffering a deficit in primary experiences – that which we can see, feel, taste, hear and smell for ourselves. Certainly this strikes something of a chord with me. As someone who spent most waking hours of my early childhood playing outdoors, catching grasshoppers with my bare hands, climbing trees, building dens and exploring the woods, I appreciate how nature's many wonders can capture a child's imagination.

But despite the fact that woodland, fields and streams can provide an abundance of excitement, and wondrous places to explore, children who grow up in cities – and maybe never get the chance to climb trees or catch insects – do not suffer from a disorder of any kind. Children can have hours of fun on street corners, in back gardens or in local parks – kicking a ball around, scrambling to the top of climbing frames, play-fighting with their mates, and just messing around – if only they are allowed to.

The issue today is that children and young people are given less and less freedom to roam outdoors *at all*. It is undoubtedly the case that there are far fewer kids out and about on street corners or in parks unaccompanied by adults. The much-quoted UK study *One False Move* shows a dramatic decrease in children's independent mobility over the period of two decades (Hillman *et al.* 1990). Whereas, in

1971, 80 per cent of seven and eight-year-old children in England were allowed to travel to school on their own, in 1990 the figure was only 9 per cent. Figures from the Department for Transport (DfT) show that the proportion of primary school children who walked or cycled to school unaccompanied was as low as 5 per cent in 2006 (DfT 2007). Research carried out for the Home Office and Department for Education and Skills in 2003 showed that 67 per cent of eight to ten-year-olds and 24 per cent of eleven to fifteen-year-olds had never been to the park or the shops on their own (Farmer and Trikha 2005).

Similar trends are apparent in the US. A study conducted by Rhonda Clements, professor of education at Manhattanville College, indicates that outdoor play is in serious decline (Clements 2004). Eighty-five per cent of the mothers reported that their child or children played outdoors less often than a generation ago. Seventy per cent of mothers reported playing outdoors every day when they were young, compared with only 31 per cent of their children. Also, when the mothers played outdoors they stayed outdoors for longer periods: 56 per cent remained outdoors for three hours at a time or longer, compared with only 22 per cent of their children. The trade group National Sporting Goods Association and the research firm American Sports Data found spontaneous outdoor activities such as bike riding, swimming and touch football have declined dramatically in the US since 1995. Bike riding alone is down by 31 per cent over the last decade.

My sister, Karen, along with her husband and three children, were recently in London for the weekend with family friends who were visiting from Norway. Over breakfast they discussed their plans for the day. Fanny, who was soon to turn seventeen, and Marcus, almost fifteen, were not interested in traipsing around the sights of London with their parents and would rather go shopping in Camden Market on their own. Olav, Fanny's father, responded, 'Absolutely not!' 'But why not?' asked Fanny, adding, 'After all, next year I'm going Inter-railing on my own.' 'No way,' reaffirmed Olav. After a moment's silence Karen piped up that she had been seventeen when she went Inter-railing around Europe with Fanny's mother. Sheepishly Olav admitted that he was in fact only sixteen when he first went holiday-ing abroad without his parents. They all relented and let Fanny and Marcus spend the day shopping unaccompanied in London, as long as they met back at the hotel at five o'clock – which they duly did.

Research by Colin Pooley at Lancaster University confirms that the area in which children are allowed to play has shrunk over the years (Pooley 2006). In the 1940s children were allowed to roam freely over a far wider expanse. Today children are more strictly controlled by their parents: few of the young children interviewed by the researchers had dealt with many risks, and compared with earlier generations they had not had the opportunity to learn to negotiate or to deal with challenges.

However, it is important to recognize that all is not lost. The Lancaster researchers also found that, although there had been a decline in the proportion of ten and eleven-year-olds allowed to travel around on their own, more than 50 per cent of the children's trips were still taken without an adult. They included journeys that were less than one mile long, which is why their figure was higher than other research has indicated. A survey carried out by the Children's Society and the Children's Play Council in 2001 found that the street was one of the most common outdoor spaces where children played, with 27 per cent saying it was where they played most often (BBC Online 2 August 2001). Almost the same proportion of children said they played in the garden most often.

Children's outdoor play has not disappeared completely. The dis-tance youngsters are allowed to roam has decreased significantly, parents feel compelled to supervise and monitor children a lot more closely, and research does indicate that children's games have steadily moved indoors into adult-controlled environments. But children are not cooped up inside, or 'battery-raised'. The problem is a more subtle one than that.

Structured lives

It is not only that the distance children are allowed to roam outdoors has decreased over the years, but their free time is increasingly structured and controlled by adults. In his book *In Defense of Childhood* Chris Mercogliano demonstrates the extent to which children's lives are regulated and controlled in the US:

> Virtually every arena of a child's life is subject to some form of adult mediation, supervision, or control. Kids go from before-school programs to school, from school to after-school programs, and from there to a host of extracurricular lessons and organized sports ... Hyperconcern for their children's safety and development is causing mothers and fathers to monitor their kids' activities and whereabouts far more stringently than my mom ever did. Fearful that their children will be left behind once they start school, many parents also focus on formal learning at ever earlier stages.
>
> (Mercogliano 2007: xi)

In *The Power of Play* David Elkind points out that over the past decades US children have lost twelve hours of free time a week, including eight hours of unstructured play and outdoor activities. In contrast, the amount of time children spend in organized sports has doubled:

> Children are not allowed to play on their own to the extent that they once were. And much of the play they engage with is organized and run by adults. This robs children of the opportunity to innovate and learn from risk-taking behaviours. To be sure, children today still manage to play on their own, but it is now the exception and not the rule.
>
> (Elkind 2007: 80–1)

Even infants' lives are being increasingly structured, with parents obsessing about their children being given a head start in life – through 'educational' programmes such as *Baby Einstein*. US journalist Alissa Quart, author of *Hothouse Kids: the Dilemma of the Gifted Child*, notes, 'Until 1997, there were no Baby Einstein videos.

By 2003, 32 per cent of our nation's infants owned at least one Baby Einstein video' (Quart 2006a: 24).

In an article in the *Atlantic Monthly* Quart mockingly describes how children can see 'such ostensibly mind-developing scenes as the one, in *Baby Van Gogh*, where a puppet called Vincent van Goat trots through the six primary colours as they appear in van Gogh's Starry Night and Wheat Fields with Reaper at Sunrise' (Quart 2006b: 23).

Quart shows that a vast industry has expanded to guilt-trip parents into providing infants and toddlers with right kinds of educational programmes, teaching their babies sign language and testing their toddler's IQ. Parents are led to believe that they are providing their children with 'an early boost' in their cognitive development. But a number of fallacious claims about the educational value of the toys are made by the retailers, based mainly on the often quoted statements that 'the minds of infants and toddlers are developing rapidly' and 'young children are most receptive to external stimuli'.

The Baby Einstein Company is the brainchild of Julie Aigner-Clark, who was lionized by US President George W. Bush in his State of the Union address in 2007. 'With her help Baby Einstein has grown into a $200 million business. Julie represents the great enterprising spirit of America,' said the President. Never mind that it has never been established whether *Baby Einstein* has any effect at all on children's intelligence or cognitive development.

Not only are there educational tools parents can purchase to give their children a head start in life, there are major US tutoring chains, such as Sylvan Learning Systems, that have introduced pre-kindergarten tutoring services. Anxious mums and dads can send their children to several thirty-minute classes a week, where they will memorize letter charts and study flash cards. But according to Maryanne Wolf, head of Tufts University's Center for Reading and Language Research, identifying a flash card at an early age isn't reading: even 'a pigeon can do it', she told *Time* magazine (Paul 21 November 2007).

Similarly, in the UK children's nurseries are increasingly preoccupied with 'hothousing children'. Because of New Labour's excessive reliance on targets as a measure of success, children's activities in nurseries are becoming more and more structured – with their opportunity for self-directed play increasingly limited.

In March 2007 the UK government published a new framework document, *Early Years Foundation Stage* (EYFS). It aims to set the 'standards for development, learning and care of all children from birth to the age of five'. From September 2008 every registered early-years provider and school are required to follow the EYFS and monitor children's progress according to sixty-nine 'early learning goals'. It should not be too hard to appreciate that such intricate monitoring of children's behaviour and abilities is anathema to creating a challenging and enjoyable learning environment. A 'national curriculum for toddlers', as the framework document has been labelled, will reduce further the chance for young children to just play and mess around.

Unfortunately, policy advisers and policymakers are not relenting, but are pushing for further and further supervision and regulation of children and young people's lives. One of the IPPR's recommendations coming out of the report *Freedom's Orphans* is:

> Participation of every secondary school pupil (from eleven to sixteen years old) in at least two hours a week of structured and purposeful extracurricular activities – such as martial arts, drama clubs, sports, cadets and Scouts. This would take place through extended school hours of between 8.00 a.m. and 6.00 p.m. and would involve a legal extension of the school day. Parents who did not ensure their child attended two hours a week of activities might ultimately be fined, in the same way as parents are punished for their child's persistent truancy.
>
> (IPPR 6 November 2006)

Risk aversion

How have we ended up in a situation where children spend more and more of their time in adult-supervised environments – and that is assumed to be a good thing?

Part of the blame for this trend must lie at the door of politicians and policymakers, whose lack of faith in parents' ability to socialize their own children is coupled with their increasing fixation on target-oriented achievement. This takes place in the context of a generalized sense of anxiety and risk aversion, particularly when it comes to children. US historian Peter Stearn, author of *Anxious Parents: A History of Modern Childrearing in America*, told me that parents encourage children – even in their late teens or early twenties – to wait for their guidance and not to take enough initiative and responsibility. 'In my view,' says Stearn, 'parents, encouraged by experts and popularizers, have come to regard kids as excessively fragile.' Parents feel more and more strongly that kids need protection rather than being allowed to roam freely. The result is, he says, that 'some kids never really manage to cut the psychological apron strings'.

But it is not only parents who are the conduits of fear: schools also are becoming increasingly risk-averse. Early in 2007 the BBC reported that St John's Primary School near Lincoln had banned traditional playground games like kiss-chase and tag because of the risk of children running into each other and getting hurt. Many were outraged, referring to it as Health and Safety gone mad. But this is not an isolated incident. A number of schools in the UK had already implemented similar bans and more and more elementary schools in the US are prohibiting traditional games.

In 2002 Hampden Gurney Primary School in west London, described as 'a twenty-first-century architectural classic', was shortlisted for the prestigious Royal Institute of British Architects' (RIBA) Stirling Prize. From the outside it looks more like a swanky office building than a school. There is no conventional playground. Instead each of its six floors – one for each year group – has a play deck made of rubber. Teachers can therefore ensure children of particular age groups play together, insulated from hard surfaces and contact with differently aged children. We are told that this has dramatically reduced the number of accidents. But at what price?

'It is frightening to imagine that this is the primary school of the future,' Julian Grenier, head teacher of a nursery centre in London, has written on *spiked*:

> This will be a future for children in which they are even more constrained and controlled. They will be deprived of joyous, ordinary experiences like getting rained on, feeling the wind, playing outside, organising games, sitting under trees and digging in sandpits ... So there is nowhere left for the children to play football. Nowhere where brothers, sisters and friends in different classes can meet up at playtime.
>
> (Grenier 3 December 2002)

The drive to reduce risks in children's lives has been relentless. Both in the UK and the US diving boards have disappeared from many swimming pools. Many new pools do not have deep ends. 'If children are lucky,' Mercogliano writes in *In Defense of Childhood*, 'a permissive lifeguard might let them jump into the water' (Mercogliano 2007: xiii). A couple of years ago an acquaintance of mine told me she wanted to teach her children to dive. Diving was one of her passions as a child. 'But I had to take them on a family holiday to Sweden to give them a chance to practise,' she said. She had not found a swimming pool in London with diving boards that children were permitted to use.

The Scottish campaign group Generation Youth Issues in 2007 launched a campaign called 'Cotton-wool kids can't swim', aiming to abolish the irrational 'safe swimming' policies being adopted by councils across Scotland. Many pools are taking an overly cautious approach and are refusing entry to some parents and children for 'health and safety' reasons. One father, for example, was turned away with his two toddlers from Bellahouston swimming pool because the pool's policy demands a ratio of one adult to one child for children under the age of four. As Stuart Waiton, Chair of Generation Youth Issues, says: 'Child safety simply appears to swamp all other considerations and turn those providing these services into risk managers and insurance clerks rather than providers of public services' (Generation Youth Issues 26 November 2007).

Children's fears

It is not only adult control that is restricting children's freedom to roam. Children have internalized many adult concerns. Bob Reitemeier, chief executive of the Children's Society, warned in 2007:

> If we go too far down the road of being overprotective and not allowing children to explore, to play, to be up with their peers, but also with children of other ages, then we may be influencing the way in which they look at society and social interaction later on.
> (BBC Online 5 June 2007)

Indeed, researchers from Lancaster University found that today's primary school-age children voice a number of concerns about playing outside unsupervised – in particular about being abducted or run over. What a contrast with respondents who had been the same age in the 1940s, who recalled how they 'swam in dirty canals and played in air raid shelters and did not tell their parents about encounters with "flashers"' (Pooley 2006).

A survey of 800 children aged between four and sixteen carried out by the Children's Society and the Children's Play Council in 2001 found that 25 per cent were put off playing outside for fear of being bullied by older children, and 17 per cent felt unable to play outdoors because of the dangers of traffic (BBC Online 2 August 2001). *A Child's Place*, a report by the think-tank Demos and the Green Alliance, found that children are keen to spend more time out of the house but are often too frightened to do so – associating being outdoors with danger (Thomas and Thompson 2004).

But not all children are fearful. A two-year study by the Child Accident Prevention Trust (CAPT) examined how youngsters in the relatively deprived metropolitan borough of Gateshead in Tyne and Wear perceive their exposure to risk during play (CAPT 2002).

Surveying 2,000 young people aged eleven to fourteen, they found that the most popular places to play and hang around in were friends' homes, followed by local streets, cafés, parks and shopping centres. Many viewed security guards and closed circuit television (CC-TV) positively because it made places feel safer for them. But 40 per cent of the children actively sought out more 'dangerous places' such as wasteland, building sites, subways or underpasses, rivers, abandoned buildings and quarries. They enjoyed visiting such places because it allowed them to escape adult supervision, posed exciting challenges, such as being chased by security guards, and gave them a place of your own – like building their own den. Children do not respond in a uniform way to today's culture of fear.

Surveillance society

Unsettled by the perceived plethora of risks faced by their children, many parents are searching for ever more intrusive ways of monitoring their children's lives. The Future Foundation report *The Changing Face of Parenting* claims that over two-thirds of parents of young children are extremely worried about their children's well-being and future, leading to support for various novel surveillance technologies – particularly among newer, more technology-savvy parents (Future Foundation 2006). Video links to school or nursery are considered useful by one in three parents with children born in 2000 or later, as compared with one in ten of those with children born in 1989 or earlier. In addition, 41 per cent of these newer parents would be interested in location-tracking devices for their children.

Webcams in nurseries and pre-schools have existed in the US for well over a decade. Companies such as WatchMeGrow and Kindercam have offered parents the possibility of watching the activities of their child 'live' in the nursery or pre-school while they themselves are at work. Such webcams have also been introduced into some nurseries in the UK.

This drive towards closer and closer supervision and surveillance extends into adolescence. Children and young people's privacy is frequently invaded in the name of protection. In 2007 it was reported that half of UK parents log on to networking web sites to spy on their children's activities on those sites. According to the help line Parentline Plus, mums and dads snoop around the sites their children visit in order to check up on them (Bennett 21 May, 2007). A couple of years earlier a study by Sonia Livingstone, Professor of Social Psychology at the London School of Economics, found that a quarter of parents checked their children's e-mail (Livingstone 2005). In the past, reading a child's diary would be seen as an unacceptable invasion of a child's privacy and a fundamental breach of trust. Today many parents are positively encouraged to spy on their children.

As Richard Woods reported in the *Sunday Times*:

> Modern devices enable parents to see infants on video links; to track older children from a distance; monitor internet use secretly; read deleted text messages; listen in to mobile phone calls; find out if their teenagers are driving too fast; or even tell what their children have spent their school lunch money on.
>
> (Woods 20 May 2007)

In this climate of hyper-surveillance it is a wonder that children ever gain the independence to do anything. Contrast the cocooned world of the modern child with the 1950s childhood recalled by the American writer Bill Bryson:

> Kids were always outdoors – I knew kids who were pushed out the back door at eight in the morning and not allowed back in until five unless they were on fire or actively bleeding – and they were always looking for something to do. If you stood on any corner with a bike – any corner anywhere – over a hundred children, many of whom you had never seen before, would appear and ask you where you were going ... Life in Kid World, wherever you went, was unsupervised, unregulated and robustly – at times insanely – physical, and yet it was a remarkably peaceful place.
>
> (Bryson 2007: 63–4)

Steven Mintz provides a persuasive account in *Huck's Raft* of how, from the vantage point of human history, contemporary children's lives are more regulated and supervised than ever before. 'Far more than previous generations, we have prolonged and intensified children's emotional and psychological dependence,' he argues (Mintz 2006: x). In an effort to keep their children safe parents and teachers are ending up increasingly hemming them in.

And, as US child psychologist David Elkind, author of *The Power of Play*, points out, this is not good for kids. Elkind argues that 'children can play safely without adult organisation; they have done so as long as people have been on earth', and that we should not try to make play risk-free, 'because we learn through experience and we learn through bad experiences. Through failure we learn how to cope' (Elkind 2007: 73).

THREE

CHILDHOOD IN HISTORICAL PERSPECTIVE

If we take the word children to mean a class of people somewhere between the ages of seven and, say, seventeen, requiring special forms of nurturing and protection, and believed to be qualitatively different from adults, then there is ample evidence that children have existed for less than four hundred years.

(Neil Postman, 1994, p. xi)

US historian Steven Mintz stresses how much more capable, adaptable and resilient children are than is often assumed by society today:

Historically the young have been exposed to the stresses of child labour, neglect, and malnutrition. African-American children lived in slavery, history's most extreme form of dehumanisation and exploitation, followed by nearly a century of *de jure* and *de facto* discrimination. Past experience places contemporary problems of childhood and adolescence in proper perspective.

(Mintz 2006: 4)

But proper perspective is something that is sorely missing in debates about the state of children and childhood today. It is easy to forget, for example, that only a few hundred years ago children could not even be said to have a childhood. The French historian Philippe Aries argued in his classic book *Centuries of Childhood: A Social History of Family Life* that, in medieval times, 'as soon as the child could live without the constant solicitude of his mother, his nanny or his cradle-rocker, he belonged to adult society' (Aries 1973: 125). Many childhood historians have given a vivid insight into how backward and ignorant many medieval societies were – societies that lacked the ability to distinguish between children and adults. 'Children could be convicted for any of the more than two hundred crimes for which the penalty was hanging,' US critic and communications theorist Neil Postman writes in *The Disappearance of Childhood* (Postman 1994: 53). A number of historians have pointed to the example of a seven-year-old girl who, in the eighteenth century, was hanged in Norwich for the crime of stealing a petticoat.

In the Middle Ages, at the tender age of seven, children were expected to enter the adult world – where they acted, and were treated, as smaller versions of other adults. Infants under two were treated with emotional indifference, according to Aries, mainly because of the low chance of them surviving to see their second birthday. In *Huck's Raft* Steven Mintz similarly argues that in the Middle Ages infants were viewed as unformed and even animalistic because of their physical dependence on adults and their inability to speak. A parent's duty was to hurry a child towards adult status, as servants and apprentices for instance, Mintz explains.

Some historians have questioned the claim that infants were treated with emotional indifference in the Middle Ages. In *The Invention of Childhood* Hugh Cunningham writes:

> It was once thought that parents shrugged off the death of their children ... When infant and child mortality was so high, it made psychological sense, it was thought, to protect yourself against too much grief. Certainly we can find evidence of that, but the dominant tone in the writings of the literate was of anguish and a struggle to make sense of their loss.
>
> (Cunningham 2006: 70)

But Cunningham also agrees that childhood was viewed very differently in the past: 'For many people throughout history to think of childhood as the most enviable part of life would have been unimaginable. Childhood was something to be got through on the way, they hoped, to something better' (Cunningham 2006: 15).

Whether or how much parents in medieval times could be said to love their children, today's separation of a distinct world of childhood with its own clothes, games, entertainment, literature and education is undoubtedly modern. Over the past century or so the family has become increasingly focused emotionally and financially on the welfare of the child in ways that would have been unrecognizable to people in previous centuries.

'Between the 1870s and 1930s the value of American children was transformed,' Princeton University sociologist Viviana Zelizer writes in *Pricing the Priceless Child: The Changing Social Value of Children*. 'In the twentieth century the economically useless but emotionally priceless child displaced the nineteenth-century useful child' (Zelizer 1994: 209). Postman similarly sees the middle of the nineteenth century as a key turning point in the history of childhood:

> The period between 1850 and 1950 represents the high water mark of childhood ... In a hundred laws children were classified as qualitatively different from adults; in a hundred customs, assigned a preferred status and offered protection from the vagaries of adult life.
>
> (Postman 1994: 67)

This is in marked contrast to the Middle Ages. 'Medieval civilisation had forgotten the *paideia* of the ancients and knew nothing as yet of modern education,' explains Aries (1973: 20). That is, the Greek concept of a higher type of person – created through education and study, to produce a well rounded, fully educated citizen – did not exist in the Middle Ages. According to Neil Postman it was the birth of the printing press that led to the emergence of a literate society and, with that, the idea of adulthood and childhood. 'Medieval behaviour was characterized by childishness among all age groups,' he writes (Postman 1994: 30), but 'from print onward, adulthood had to be earned. It became a symbolic, not a biological, achievement' (Postman 1994: 36). He adds, 'Because the school was designed for preparation of a literate adult, the young came to be perceived not as miniature adults but as something quite different altogether – unformed adults' (Postman 1994: 41).

Social historians have shown that communication in the Middle Ages was almost exclusively oral – that is, spoken. It is a period in history where books seem to have vanished out of sight. Evidence indicates that some private tutoring existed, and some schools could be found in monasteries, but there was no systematic means of teaching the population to read and write. In such a society, Postman argues, there cannot be a concept of an adult and, therefore, nor can there be a concept of a child: 'Immersed in an oral world, living in the same social sphere as adults, unrestrained by segregating institutions, the medieval child would have had access to almost all of the forms of behaviour common to the culture' (Postman 1994: 15).

Aries also emphasizes that in the Middle Ages there was no restriction on what was permitted in children's presence, whether it be coarse language or salacious actions. British historian John Plumb shows that adults and children in medieval times did not occupy separate worlds: 'The coarse village festivals depicted by Brueghel, showing men and women besotted with drink, groping for each other with unbridled lust, have children eating and drinking with adults' (Plumb 1971: 7).

So what changed for society to adopt such a radically different view of its young? Of course, as Postman argues, the printing press and the emergence of a literate society were important, but that is not the whole story. We need to look beyond one form of technology to broader political and economic factors to understand the revolutionary changes that took place. The Enlightenment brought about a radically new conception of human beings: the idea that individuals are autonomous and rational, should have rights and responsibilities, and are capable of participating in political life, came to fruition during this time. It was this conception of human beings that brought about the distinction between adults and children.

Beyond the Dark Ages

The modern view of childhood is understood to have been built upon the ideas of two great philosophers, John Locke and Jean-Jacques Rousseau. Locke's idea of a *tabula rasa* – the mind as a blank slate at birth – presents adults with the responsibility for 'what is eventually written on the mind', writes Postman (Postman 1994: 57). From the Lockean conception comes the view of the child as an 'unformed person who through literacy, education, reason, self-control, and shame may be made into a civilized adult' (Postman 1994: 59). Rousseau, on the other hand, put forward the Romantic view of the child – highlighting the charm and value of children, arousing 'a curiosity about the nature of childhood that persists to this present day' (Postman 1994: 58).

Locke's view of the child is generally seen to be in conflict with that held by Rousseau, and this is often used as the basis for the rather hackneyed debates over 'nature versus nurture'. Locke's notion of a *tabula rasa* is taken to imply that children have to be civilized, or taught how to be human, while the Romantic view is seen as indicating that children are naturally virtuous and have to be protected from the corrupting influence of adult society. But what is important is that both present an image of children as different from adults, and both stress the importance of education in one form or another.

Postman argues that the idea of the child 'as schoolboy or schoolgirl whose self and individuality must be preserved by nurturing, whose capacity for self-control, deferred gratification, and logical thought must be extended, whose knowledge of life must be under the control of adults' emanates from the Lockean perspective (Postman 1994: 63). Yet, at the same time, the Romantic view of childhood advocates that 'the child is understood as having its own rules for development, and a charm, curiosity, and exuberance that must not be strangled' (Postman 1994: 63). Rousseau was one of the first to criticize educational methods that solely presented ideas and materials from an adult point of view. In his classic text *Emile*, first published in 1762, Rousseau wrote, 'Childhood has its own ways of seeing, thinking, and feeling which are proper to it. Nothing is less sensible than to want to substitute ours for theirs' (Rousseau 1979: 90).

The concept of the child that emerged in the Enlightenment was based on the idea that children are fundamentally different from adults, that children are not born into adulthood but must achieve it, and that it is the responsibility of adults to both protect children and lead them down the road to adulthood. But even during the Enlightenment most children did not have what we would call a childhood. This is because childhood is not just an idea. It is a hard-earned historical achievement. For much of the eighteenth and nineteenth centuries people did not have much choice but to treat children as little adults.

Only in the late nineteenth and early twentieth centuries, with the drastic decline in child labour and the advent and extension of compulsory schooling, could childhood really be said to exist in the modern sense. It was not until the 1870 Education Act, which gave rise to a national system of state education, that schooling became a priority in the UK. Before that, in the eighteenth and nineteenth centuries, children as young as six years of age would have to work long hours – longer than many adults would put up with today – in atrocious working conditions. They often contracted debilitating diseases and suffered terrible injuries. Accidental amputations were common in factories, when children, who were small enough to reach into the factory machinery, would attempt to clean the parts or clear obstructions. Young chimney sweeps suffered from chronic breathing problems and often broken and deformed limbs.

Karl Marx's *Capital* graphically describes the working conditions of children in nineteenth-century Britain. He quotes a *Daily Telegraph* article from January 1860 that describes employment in the lace trade:

Children of nine or ten years are dragged from their squalid beds at two, three, or four o'clock in the morning and compelled to work for a bare subsistence until ten, eleven or twelve at night, their limbs wearing away, their frames dwindling, their faces whitening, and their humanity absolutely sinking into stone-like torpor.

(Marx 1983 :233)

Conditions were equally dire in the potteries of Staffordshire:

William Wood, nine years old, was seven years and ten months when he began to work. He 'ran moulds' (carried ready-moulded articles into the drying room, afterwards bringing back the empty mould) from the beginning. He came to work every day in the week at 6.00 a.m. and left off about 9.00 p.m.

(Marx 1983: 234)

The work was not only exhausting, but debilitating. Quoting a senior physician at North Staffordshire Infirmary, Marx writes:

[Potters] are, as a rule, stunted in growth, ill-shaped and frequently ill-formed in the chest; they become prematurely old, and are certainly short-lived: they are phlegmatic and bloodless, and exhibit their debility of conditions by obstinate attacks of dyspepsia, and disorders of the liver and kidneys, and by rheumatism. But of all the diseases they are especially prone to chest-disease, to pneumonia, phthisis, bronchitis, and asthma.

(Marx 1983: 235)

Marx is by no means the only person to have detailed the immiseration of the British working class during the industrial revolution, though he does it more eloquently than most. A friend of mine, who grew up in Staffordshire in the 1980s, recalls that discussions of the levels of death and danger facing children working in the mills and other industries formed a large part of her school history lessons. To look back on those times, from the privileged, protected position of children today requires an extraordinary leap of the imagination.

In the US, Steven Mintz shows how Hannibal, the small Mississippi riverfront town where Mark Twain grew up, and which 'holds a special place in the American collective imagination', was 'anything but a haven of stability and security' (Mintz 2006: 1). '[O]ur cherished myth about childhood as a bucolic time of freedom, untainted innocence, and self-discovery comes to life in this river town,' writes Mintz – even though in mid-nineteenth-century Hannibal a quarter of the children died before their first birthday and half before their twenty-first.

Even today there are children around the world who do not have much of a childhood. When living and training in a Thai boxing (Muay Thai) camp in Koh Samui, Thailand, I met many children who had to fend not just for themselves but also for their extended families. One boy, Jook, then fifteen years of age, had joined the camp when he was twelve. He never knew his mother, and his father died when he was only ten, leaving him to be brought up by his grandmother. Before joining the camp Jook worked in the building trade, starting work at 6.00 a.m. every day, including Sundays, and working 'until the job was done'. He earned 2,000 bhat (less than £40) a month, on which he had to support himself, his grandmother and his two sisters. Joining the Muay Thai camp had given Jook the chance to earn more money. He told me he often had to train and fight when he didn't want to, and was affectionately known as 'lazy Jook' in the camp – despite training many hours a day and having sixty-eight professional fights under his belt. His exceptional speed and agility allowed him to get away with a little less training than the average fighter. But, according to Jook, 'Even if I don't want to, I have to fight. I need the money.' Financial pressure meant he had little choice but to enter the ring week in, week out.

Ceri Dingle, Director of the youth education charity Worldwrite, describes meeting children as young as twelve heading households in Ghana: a country with which Worldwrite has organized several youth exchange programmes. 'Young children are clearly capable of far more than we imagine in our over-protected West,' she remarks. Even though, as Dingle says, 'toil in the home, or looking after your family, is not something you'd want youngsters to be obliged to do', it is a sobering thought to recognize that in some parts of the world children can, and have to, do these things, simply because they lack the basic opportunities that children in the developed world can take for granted.

The disappearance of childhood?

Neil Postman's thought-provoking account of the emergence of childhood indicates how important it is to situate discussions about children firmly within a broader historical context. His thesis that in the present day childhood is 'disappearing' because of the role played by television sits rather uncomfortably with this broader, holistic approach.

Postman assumes that with the rise of television, which 'not only requires no skills but develops no skills' (Postman 1994: 79), modern society is rendering 'irrelevant those "traditional skills" on which literacy rests' (Postman 1994: 119). Also, with television the basis of an 'information hierarchy' collapses, he argues, there is no longer knowledge that is exclusively for adults. The end result is that children are unambiguously treated as adults in today's society.

Furthermore, he argues, 'There is no more obvious symptom of the merging of children's and adult's values and styles than what is happening with children's games, which is to say, they are disappearing' (Postman 1994: 129). Children no longer just kick a ball around but their games have become like adult games – official and 'mock-professional'.

There are some major flaws in this argument. Play may be more structured, but children's games have not disappeared. The television is ubiquitous, and the 'visual literacy' it requires may well be inferior to the literacy demanded by books, but society has not abandoned the need for education – let alone reading. The Lockean and Rousseauian concept of the child as in need of education still persists, and though there are problems with modern education, it is still considered important that children learn things at school. And although society has in many ways lost the ability to differentiate between children and adults, the concept of childhood has not *disappeared*. Today's children are still seen as different from adults and in need of a special kind of care and protection – in many ways, even more so than before.

Today's attitude to children is much more ambiguous than Postman recognizes. But Postman is right to the extent that there is a tendency for society to treat children as adults. Even though children are seen as excessively fragile and in constant need of care and protection, much of their behaviour at the same time is viewed through the prism of adult behaviour. The case of the ten-year-old boy in Manchester, England, who was charged in 2006 with a racially aggravated public order offence for calling another schoolboy a 'Paki' is an extreme example of this. As I explore further in Chapter 6, many anti-bullying campaigns show the same lack of ability to appreciate that children are children.

Following one of the most shocking murders of the 1990s, the English law was changed to reflect society's unease about the distinction between adults and children. The killing of two-year-old James Bulger by two ten-year-old boys, Robert Thompson and Jon Venables, in 1993 led to a deluge of media hand wringing and political gesture making. Then Conservative Prime Minister John Major announced, 'We must condemn a little more, and understand a little less,' while the Labour Party's shadow Ministers damned the modern 'excuse culture'. A few years later, the newly elected New Labour government passed the 1998 Crime and Disorder Act, which abolished the presumption of *doli incapax* – that is, the presumption that a child under fourteen years of age does not understand that what they have done is 'seriously wrong', rather than 'just naughty'.

Novelist Blake Morrison, whose insightful book *As if* reflected in detail on the Bulger trial, wrote in the *Guardian* in 2003, 'Amid the hysteria in 1993, Thompson and Venables lost the right to be seen as children, or even as human' (Morrison 6 February 2003). The message of the Bulger case, Morrison points out, 'was that we were living in a violent new world, where you couldn't trust your children with anyone, not even other children'. Even though, as Morrison explains, child homicides remain extremely rare: whatever the perception, in reality we have not 'bred a new generation of child-monsters'.

Family therapist Michael Ungar points out that Canada and the US are similarly seeing what is described as 'up-criming', a phenomenon 'where our children are more likely than ever before to be charged and tried for adult offenses that would have been seen as nothing more than children misbehaving twenty years ago' (Ungar 2007: 106).

In the distant past, people had no choice but to treat children as little adults. Now that we have a more advanced society, it is up to us to protect childhood as an important stage of development rather than pathologizing it as a dangerous, unhappy time; and to help children on their way into adulthood, rather than seeking to keep them infantile for ever.

PART II

FREEDOM AND CHILD DEVELOPMENT

FOUR

GROWING UP
Why risk-taking is good for kids

Adulthood is the ever-shrinking period between childhood and old age.
It is the apparent aim of modern industrial societies to reduce this period
to a minimum.
(Thomas Szasz, prominent US psychiatrist in the antipsychiatry movement)

When I was a child in Norway outdoor activities were encouraged
from an early age. A childhood with no broken bones was said to be
a 'no-good childhood'. I was free to roam around my neighbourhood
long before I even started school. The local children, my siblings and
I built dens, climbed trees and played in the woods and by the sea. As
long as we were back for our evening meal we could stay out as long
as we liked. We created our own little fantasy worlds, sometimes
scaring each other near to death. My sisters and I even took it upon
ourselves to provide burial sites in our back garden for all the dead
animals we came across in our neighbourhood – cats, birds, frogs or
even snails. I hope we were aware enough to know it was best not to
touch the dead animals with our bare hands, but I cannot be sure
about it. There were many arguments and many tears were spilt. But
the richness of the experience we gained from the freedom we were
given above all involved a lot of fun and excitement.

The commitment to unsupervised outdoor play was put to the test in Norway several years ago, after the tragic death of Silje, a five-year-old-girl, in my home town of Trondheim. Silje's death stunned Norway. In October 1994 she was beaten by three boys of her own age, knocked unconscious and left to freeze to death. Playing outside in the snow, a game clearly went seriously out of hand. The boys ran away in fear when Silje lay on the ground motionless, having 'stopped crying'.

If they only had alerted an adult earlier Silje could have been alive today. Her injuries were minor. She died of hypothermia. But the boys did not inform an adult until it was too late. Questions were asked in the national and international press about where the adults were at the time. Should a five-year-old be left to play outside unsupervised in freezing temperatures? However, a popular and media consensus quickly emerged that the risk of serious accidents, which is extremely small, is worth taking in order to allow the vast majority of children a healthy and rich childhood. Norwegians have a special love of outdoor pursuits. They are therefore very reluctant to restrict children's freedom to roam outdoors – without adults watching them – to the same extent as other nations do.

Even in the UK the debate about dealing with the risks of children's play has started to shift. In November 2007 Tom Mullarkey, chief executive of the Royal Society for the Prevention of Accidents (RoSPA), warned against wrapping children in cotton wool. The head of a charity that normally raises the red flag about children having accidents made a very sensible comment:

> A skinned knee or a twisted ankle in a challenging and exciting play environment is not just acceptable, it is a positive necessity in order to educate our children and to prepare them for a complex, dangerous world, in which healthy, robust activity is more a national need than ever before.
>
> (RoSPA 2007: 7)

Accidental injuries are the leading cause of death among children under fifteen years of age in the US. More than 5,600 young lives are lost every year, and as the National Safe Kids Campaign (NSKC) points out, that is an average of fifteen children each day (NSKC 2003). In fact, as UNICEF points out, accidental injury is 'the principal cause of child death in all developed nations – accounting for almost 40 per cent of deaths in the age group one to fourteen' (UNICEF 2001: 4). But it should also be pointed out that the number of child fatalities from accidental injury fell by about 50 per cent in OECD nations between 1970 and 1995, and the UK has one of the lowest rates in the world (UNICEF 2001). Of course accident prevention work should continue in order to reduce the number of child fatalities further. But Mullarkey is right when stating that things should be 'as safe as necessary, not as safe as possible' (RoSPA 2007:13).

Earlier in 2007 David Yearly, Play Safety Manager of the RoSPA, wrote in the publication *Cotton Wool Kids*:

> The ability to judge risks as adults is not something that we simply acquire at the age of majority. It is a skill that is learnt through exposure to hazards. When as adults, we encounter a new hazard or risk, we apply those skills that we learnt as children to the situation.
>
> (Jones 2007: 15)

RoSPA is calling for an intelligent debate about how we manage risk today, especially the risks facing children.

It seems that the burgeoning risk industry has begun to wake up to the fact that the zealousness with which some public bodies have banned potentially hazardous childhood games and toys, from balloons to snowball fights, has started to raise some eyebrows. And so it is feeling the need to respond. Aiming to jettison its killjoy reputation, the UK Health and Safety Executive (HSE), which is responsible with local governments for the enforcement of health and safety regulation, has started publishing and challenging 'myths of the month' online. The September 2007 Myth of the Month was 'Kids must wear goggles to play conkers'. 'This is one of the oldest chestnuts around, a truly classic myth,' states the HSE web site:

A well-meaning head teacher decided children should wear safety goggles to play conkers. Subsequently some schools appear to have banned conkers on 'health & safety' grounds or made children wear goggles, or even padded gloves! Realistically the risk from playing conkers is incredibly low and just not worth bothering about. If kids deliberately hit each other over the head with conkers, that's a discipline issue, not health and safety.

The UK Institution of Occupational Safety and Health (IOSH) has also started voicing its concern about the current obsession with safety. Lisa Fowlie, President of IOSH, says: 'Health and safety is sometimes used as an excuse – it's easier to ban something completely than to find a way to let it go ahead' (Sky News, 13 October 2007). Going a few steps further than the HSE, the IOSH sponsored the 2007 World Conker Championships.

Health and Safety executives, along with government departments, have been forced to consider what many play-professionals have argued for some time – the importance of risk taking during play. Mike Greenaway, Director of Play Wales, for instance, has been vocal in voicing his concern about today's 'bubble-wrap culture' where children are not given the opportunity to learn how to deal with danger. 'It is desperately important that children can take risks,' he told me. So, for instance, 'we do not know we are cycling too fast until we fall off and hurt ourselves, and learn that we should be going around the corner more slowly'.

Due to concerns about society's excessive risk aversion, the HTI, a leading UK broker between business and education, has launched a national scheme called Go4it to award schools that are 'developing a risk-positive climate that promotes innovation in a number of ways and over a period of time' (Jones 2007: 30). In the HTI publication *Cotton Wool Kids* Sir Digby Jones, HTI President and former Director General of the Confederation of British Industry (CBI), asks:

What messages are we communicating to young people when we attempt to eliminate every last vestige of risk from the curriculum, sport, play, home life and social life? Have we reached the stage where the only place children are able to take a risk is in the safe virtual reality of a computer screen?

(Jones 2007: 9)

According to Jones the playground is no longer a place where children can take risks. The message children are given, he writes, is 'Don't play conkers in the playground, you might get hurt; don't do backstroke in the swimming pool, you might bang into somebody; don't skip, run, throw snowballs, play on the ice, do handstands or cartwheels' (Jones 2007: 11). All these activities have, according to Jones, come under the axe in schools somewhere in our country, undermining children's opportunity to learn to manage risks.

Playground panics: a lesson in problematizing risk

How did we get to the situation in the first place where risk was seen as bad for children rather than something they needed to learn to deal with as a part of growing up? In *No Fear: Growing up in a Risk-averse Society* author Tim Gill, former Director of the Children's Play Council (now Play England), raises some crucial questions about risk-aversion and the impact it has on children's lives (Gill 2007). As Gill rightly points out, 'Activities and experiences that previous generations of children enjoyed without a second thought have been labelled as troubling or dangerous, while the adults who permit them are branded irresponsible' (Gill 2007:10).

The principal chapter in Gill's book takes a long hard look at the discouragingly dull nature of British school playgrounds. Increasingly, children's play has been severely curtailed and restricted by society's exaggerated sense of fear. According to Gill, the rot set in after an episode of the BBC entertainment/consumer activist show *That's Life* in May 1990. The show's presenters covered a campaign launched by a member of Parliament to make safety surfacing a legal requirement in all British playgrounds, focusing in particular on the case of an eight-year-old girl who died after falling from a swing and hitting her head on the tarmac below.

Quite quickly, in the wake of this campaign, playground providers felt compelled to introduce impact-absorbing surfacing. But research in to the prevalence of playground injuries, carried out by David Ball, a professor of risk management at Middlesex University, revealed that these safety measures did not result in a decrease in the number of accidents. Accident rates were steady between 1988 and 2002 despite the introduction of new safety standards and the spread of impact-absorbing surfacing. In fact, as Gill writes, 'A growing number of experts think that the rubber safety surfacing most often used in the UK may lead to more broken arms than other types of surface' (Gill 2007: 29).

After this initial safety-surfacing hysteria, attitudes towards play-ground safety seem to have become more relaxed in recent years. There is a new climate, says Gill, 'in which providers can build less safety-oriented, more challenging playgrounds' (Gill 2007: 38). It is to be hoped that he is right. But even so, there is still a long way to go.

A few years back Asbjørn Flemmen, a head teacher in Skudeneshavn, Norway, pioneered the building of a school playground that posi-tively encourages potentially dangerous 'thrill seeking'. And there clearly were dangers – resulting in a couple of broken bones, mainly when the playground first opened. The aim of the playground, with its many activity areas, such as the jungle, 'hut building' and 'hide and seek', was to maximize spontaneous, unsupervised play. Adults were encouraged to back off at all times. The reason for this was the recog-nition that play challenges children's existing levels of competence and, through taking risks, develops new skills.

Even in a UK climate that welcomes 'more challenging play-grounds' I doubt this kind of playground would pass a Health and Safety inspection. Nor would the playground meet the approval of the US National Program for Playground Safety (NPPS), which describes itself as 'the premier non-profit organisation in the United States delivering training and services about outdoor play and safety'. According to the NPPS a SAFE playground is one that is created around four basic principles: Supervision; Age-appropriate equipment design; Fall surfacing; Equipment and surfacing maintenance. Adults, they advise, should provide supervision at all times. The equipment, no matter how expensive or how 'safe', can still present risks, parents are told.

Even when UK government departments and official bodies are bending over backwards to protest the need for healthy risk taking among children they still cannot quite let go of the orthodoxy of 'safety first'. In July 2007 the government launched a consultation document on where to draw the balance between protection and freedom. Ed Balls, Secretary of State for Children, Schools and Families, announced:

'Staying Safe' will be the start of a very important debate about what we all need to do – parents, politicians, employers, practitioners, children and young people – to ensure the safety and wellbeing of every child. ... We want them to be protected from harm and abuse. [But] we cannot wrap children in cotton wool – this is not protecting children. It denies them vital opportunities to learn and develop. It stunts their independence and will impede on their abilities to navigate risks for themselves as they grow up.

(Balls, 23 July 2007)

So far, so good. But a mere few months after having warned against 'wrapping children in cotton wool' Ed Balls launched the government's ten-year Children's Plan, *Building Brighter Futures*. Emphasizing its commitment to 'safe play', Balls announced that in order to 'create more safe places to play' the government would invest £225 million in play facilities over the next three years (DCSF 2007a: 31). Doing a quick search on the document showed that the word 'safe' was used 208 times. The money, Balls outlined, would fund improvements in existing playgrounds, the creation of 'thirty new pilots of supervised play parks' and provide training to 'enable 4,000 play workers to achieve recognized play qualifications' (DCSF 2007a: 31).

Note the emphasis on supervision and regulation. Children, it seems, cannot just get on with playing and making their own fun today, they need to be monitored, supervised and taught how to play.

The dangers of 'safety first'

The irony is that the increasing concern with health and safety, particularly over the last two decades, has gone hand in hand with children becoming healthier and safer than ever before. For a start, more of them stay alive. At the turn of the twentieth century 150 in every 1,000 babies born in the UK and 100 in every 1,000 babies born in the US died before they reached their first birthday. Nutrition was poor and lack of vaccinations led to deaths from smallpox, diphtheria, measles, typhoid and cholera – among many other diseases. Children are now being immunized against most of these diseases, and significant medical advances over the past decades have led to improved rates of survival for children diagnosed with cancer. Today, the infant mortality rate has dropped to five in every 1,000 babies born in the UK and seven in every 1,000 babies born in the US.

As the influential 2007 UNICEF report on child well-being in rich countries states:

> By almost any available measure, the great majority of children born into today's developed societies enjoy unprecedented levels of health and safety. Almost within living memory, one child in every five in the cities of Europe could be expected to die before his or her fifth birthday; today that risk is less than one in a hundred. Loss of life among older children is even more uncommon; fewer than one in every 10,000 young people die before the age of 19 as a result of accident, murder, suicide or violence. This, too, represents an historically unheard of level of safety.
>
> (UNICEF 2007: 15)

Figures from the US Department of Health and Human Services' Centers for Disease Control and Prevention (CDC) show that the accidental death rate among children under fifteen years of age in the US declined by 39 per cent between 1987 and 2000. In 2000 the leading cause of death from accidents among this age group was motor vehicle occupancy (28 per cent), followed by drowning (16 per cent), airway obstruction (14 per cent) and being a pedestrian (12 per cent).

Children still have accidents. Common sense tells us that children, especially toddlers, are not particularly adept at handling risks, due to their natural curiosity, coupled with a complete lack of nous. The extent of their vulnerability is borne out by UK accident and emergency (A&E) statistics. Figures from RoSPA show that almost 4,000 people die every year from accidents in the home and 2.7 million turn up at A&E Departments. Of those seeking treatment, children under four years are by far the highest-risk group, accounting for 17.4 per cent of all A&E visits. Airway obstruction is the leading injury killer in this age group, accounting for nearly 60 per cent of unintentional-injury deaths. Confronted with awareness of the potential dangers posed to their loved ones in and around the home, it is understandable that parents try to keep them safe from accidental harm.

But we have to accept that children do, and always will have, accidents. It is often more traumatic for the adults in their midst than for the children themselves. And, in trying to prevent children from having accidents, parents can deny them the freedom they need to develop. As Canadian social worker and family therapist Michael Ungar, author of *Too Safe for their own Good: How Risk and Responsibility Help Teens Thrive*, argues: 'Well-founded worry conveys to children they are loved; senseless, ungrounded worry debilitates children in ways far worse than the few bumps and bruises they may experience without us' (Ungar 2007: xii).

Overprotection can never eliminate the risks facing children – but it can bring some new risks of its own. What about, for example, the reaction to the measles, mumps and rubella (MMR) vaccine? Panicked by unproved allegations that this vaccine poses a risk, many parents refused to immunize their children – potentially exposing all children to the far greater danger of contracting measles, mumps or rubella.

Also, by diminishing children's capacity to deal with danger, overprotection could be seen to increase the risks they face when they do get let out into the wider world. Road accidents provide a salient example here. The UNICEF report on deaths by injury in rich nations shows that traffic accident fatalities account for 41 per cent of all accidental child deaths (UNICEF 2001). Still, despite large increases in traffic volume, child traffic deaths have fallen dramatically over the last decades. In England and Wales between 1985 and 2003 the pedestrian mortality rate for children under 14 years of age fell by 80 per cent. For cyclists of the same age the fatality rate fell by 73 per cent, and for car occupants by 59 per cent (Sonkin 2006).

This indicates that the roads are getting a lot safer. But as the UNICEF report points out, the fall in pedestrian death rates could be partly due to a corresponding decrease in children's exposure to traffic (UNICEF 2001). Fewer and fewer children are allowed out and about on their own. Whereas the average mileage children travelled by car increased by 70 per cent between 1985 and 2003 in the UK, the average mileage travelled on foot declined by 19 per cent, and the average mileage cycled declined by 58 per cent. So it could indeed be argued that children are safer precisely because they are not exposed to traffic to the same extent as children were in the past – despite there being many more cars on the roads.

Insulating children from traffic, however, exposes a potential danger of its own. The car is an increasingly popular form of transport for the majority of people, and there is a lot more traffic on the roads today than three decades ago: that is unlikely to change. Of course, measures can be taken to try to reduce traffic in built-up areas, as well as introducing more cycle lanes and pedestrian access. But ultimately children do need to learn to cross the road. Indeed, one could argue that they are now so insulated from traffic that they are not becoming sufficiently 'street-wise' when it comes to crossing the road on their own.

Department for Transport (DfT) figures show a recent small increase in child pedestrian death rates in the UK. The AA and other motoring organizations have warned that this increase could be the result of children having been prevented from becoming 'street-wise'. Because children are not exposed to traffic early enough they are not adept enough at judging the speed of cars or conscious enough of the dangers of traffic. They do not sufficiently understand the risks that cars pose. Therefore, on the rare occasion they are allowed out, they are at greater risk of being hit by a car. It could also be argued that, due to there being far fewer children out and about, drivers become less alert to the possibility of children suddenly running into the road.

Data gathered by the DfT shows a positive correlation – that is, an association – over a four-year period between the number of parents who forbid their children from crossing the road on their own and the number of child pedestrian deaths. So the proportion of parents with children aged between seven and ten who 'never allow their children to cross the road on their own' increased from 41 per cent in 2002 to 49 per cent in 2006. Over the same period, the number of road deaths among child pedestrians between seven and ten years of age rose from ten to eighteen.

Of course, correlation does not equal causation, and it is unlikely that there is one simple explanation for this recent increase in child pedestrian deaths. But Rob Gifford, Director of the Parliamentary Advisory Council for Transport Safety, could have a point when he says:

> Parents should consider whether forbidding their children from crossing the road unaccompanied is exposing them subsequently to additional risk. They may not acquire the skills they need. Children need to learn to cross the road on their own and the answer may be to encourage them to do so, initially while being watched.
>
> (Webster, 11 September 2007)

If children miss out on opportunities for developing a sense of risk and danger, and taking more and more responsibility for their own lives, they are likely to be at even greater risk when they eventually are let out in the 'big bad world' without having learnt essential skills. The US writer Hara Estroff Marano, Editor-at-large of *Psychology Today*, highlights the danger of making life easier for children in the short term: all you end up doing is making it harder for them in the long term. 'Parental anxiety has its place,' she says, 'but the way things now stand, it's not being applied wisely' (Marano 2004: 8). Parents are not giving children the chance to fail – which in the long term means they are less likely to succeed. Marano adds, 'As any innovator will tell you, success hinges less on getting everything right than on how you handle getting things wrong' (Marano 2005: 4).

Eternal youth

By putting too much onus on keeping them safe, adult society could be denying children the opportunity to grow up and face life's many challenges. For me, this is a clearer, and greater, problem than the possibility of exposing children to more potential physical dangers.

Michael Ungar argues that adults go to great lengths to protect children from the very experiences of failure children need to grow up healthy. Ungar's experience of working with troubled teenagers has convinced him that what today's youth are lacking are opportunities for risk taking and responsibility. The troubled youth that have come to him for help – whether they have grown up with many advantages or very few – have all told him that they crave adventure and responsibility. He concludes, 'We do our children no favours sheltering them from the challenges that come with living life to the full' (Ungar 2007: 23).

Ungar's argument is backed up by Rhi, a teenager from Georgia, in the US, who wrote on a BBC Online discussion forum on parental overprotection:

> I feel adults should loosen up a bit. I say this because I see a good number of people my age who are very irresponsible and don't have a clue. I realize that this is probably partly due to my age group. However, in school and at home many children are being babied. Because of this, I see a lot of people going off to college, or moving out, and they are, quite honestly, clueless. They cannot function on their own.
>
> (Coughlan, 5 June 2007)

Children and young people do need to be given gradually more freedom and responsibility so that they have the opportunities to show what they can do on their own. As Ungar argues, parents should give children the structure 'to navigate safely the period between being a child and acting like an adult'. 'It's our responsibility from the time they are little to help them embrace adventure and responsibility ...

A concerned parent provides scaffolding for growth, not just a life jacket for safety' (Ungar 2007: 4).

Ever since the birth of adolescence at the turn of the twentieth century there has been some tension between the amount of freedom adolescents aspire to and the amount that parents will allow them. The fact that some young people are still rebelling against parental overprotectiveness is positive. If they want to be given more freedom and responsibilities than adults will allow them, that indicates that there is something about adult society that is worth aspiring to. In other words, adult society is sufficiently dynamic for them to want to be part of it.

Unfortunately, the dynamic is towards keeping children locked in eternal youth for an ever increasing period, and many youngsters seem to be content with their lot. A number of large-scale studies of the life and experiences of US youth throughout the twentieth century are brought together in the book *On the Frontier of Adulthood: Theory, Research, and Public Policy*. The researchers show that adolescence has become a far more prolonged affair: 'A lengthy period before adulthood, often spanning the twenties and even extending into the thirties, is now devoted to further education, job exploration, experimentation in romantic relationships, and personal development' (University of Chicago Press 2008).

In addition, many more young people are living at home with their parents well into their twenties or even their thirties. This would have been unheard of fifty or 100 years ago. *On the Frontier of Adulthood* shows that during the first half of the twentieth century the gap between childhood and adulthood was much more brief – spanning the period from the early to the late teen years. 'By their early 20s most young people were socially recognized as adults, more or less indistinguishable from men and women in their 30s or 40s,' the researchers write (Furstenberg *et al.* 2005).

It is the responsibility of adults to prepare children for a full and independent life, not to protect them from every conceivable risk in the wider world. As US psychologist David Anderegg writes in *Worried all the Time*:

Kids need parents to love them and protect them and set limits with them, and they also need parents to get out of the way so that they can bring themselves up ... Trusting that they will make the right choices, or, if they make the wrong choices, that they will not be disastrous, is what we all have to do as parents.

(Anderegg 2003: 210)

Or, in the words of the nineteenth-century French chemist and biologist Louis Pasteur, 'When I approach a child, he inspires in me two sentiments: tenderness for what he is, and respect for what he may become. But childhood prolonged cannot remain a fairyland. It becomes a hell.'

FIVE

PLAY
WHAT IS IT GOOD FOR?

A child's greatest achievements are possible in play, achievements that tomorrow will become her basic level of real action and morality.
Lev Semenovich Vygotsky, 1978, p. 100)

Pre-school children: the power of make-believe

The Swiss polymath Jean Piaget, one of the most influential developmental psychologists of the twentieth century, spent hours observing children at play. He concluded that play lifts children's thinking to a higher level and helps them make sense of social experiences. But it is only once children start introducing 'symbols' – or make-believe – into play, Piaget argued, that it serves this function. It is only then it goes beyond the type of play that animals engage in.

'The young child during his whole first year, as well as all the animal species which play, seems to know nothing of make-believe,' Piaget wrote in *Play, Dreams and Imitation in Childhood* (Piaget 1962: 154). The type of play that does not involve symbols – like puppies 'play' biting other puppies – is what Piaget called 'practice games'.

Only in their second year of life do children start introducing make-believe into their play. But at this young age their imaginary situation is very close to reality – children basically reproduce real-life situations. So a child playing with a doll will copy what he or she has seen an adult do. Their thinking is still too limited to develop an imaginary situation that is not merely an imitation of what they have seen in real life. With development, and particularly with the emergence of language, children start creating increasingly complex make-believe scenarios.

So, once 'the symbol' is introduced into play, Piaget wrote, it 'goes far beyond practice'. Children are not merely practising at being adults but making sense of past experiences and learning to be more fully part of the world they live in. 'Even the game of dolls,' Piaget writes 'is much less a pre-exercise of the maternal instinct than an infinitely varied symbolic system' which, he shows, helps the child make sense of past experiences (Piaget 1962: 154).

The role of play in helping children make sense of relationships was also explored by the father of psychoanalysis, Sigmund Freud. In the essay *Creative Writers and Day-dreaming*, first presented as a lecture in 1907, he drew comparisons between children's make-believe play and creative writing:

> The child's best-loved and most intense occupation is with his play or games. Might we not say that every child at play behaves like a creative writer, in that he creates a world of his own, or rather, rearranges the things of his world in a new way which pleases him?
> (Freud 1908: 143)

This is a great insight. It is worth quoting Freud at some length here:

> The creative writer does the same as the child at play. He creates a world of fantasy which he takes very seriously – that is, which he invests with large amounts of emotion – while separating it sharply from reality ... The unreality of the writer's imaginative world, however, has very important consequences for the technique of his art; for many things which, if they were real, could give no enjoyment, can do so in the play of fantasy, and many

excitements which, in themselves, are actually distressing, can become a source of pleasure for the hearers and spectators at the performance of a writer's work.

(Freud 1908: 143)

Like the creative writer, children create a world of fantasy – a world that they take very seriously. They invest their fantasy world with large amounts of emotion while separating it from reality. And because it is separate from reality the exploration of even distressing emotions can be pleasurable. So fantasy play gives children the opportunity to explore different emotions, social roles and relationships, and try to make sense of their world. The adult world can be rather perplexing, even frightening, to a young child. Through imaginary play they can act out different emotional responses to situations they are not quite sure how to handle.

When my niece, Maja, was three years of age, she was overheard talking to her dolls about the special food she was going to give them to help them learn how to talk. Her elder brother, who due to a rare neurological disorder has limited language use, was at the time being given a special high-fat diet that could alter the chemical balance of his brain with some chance of improving his condition. Maja was creating a fantasy world with her dolls where she could explore emotions and issues in relation to the fact that her much-loved elder brother was somehow different from other children.

Similarly, when our niece and nephew – Natasha, four years of age, and Adam, almost three years of age – came to visit my husband and me in Birmingham in 2007 they, rather unfortunately, ended up frightened and distressed at a planetarium show we took them to in the Birmingham ThinkTank. When the lights went out and the show started Natasha was convinced the ceiling had disappeared and retreated in floods of tears to her father's lap. Adam wasn't quite so worried but was far from enamoured of the complete darkness, and kept suggesting to his mother that we should be getting back soon.

A couple of weeks later, their mother told me she overheard them playing together, talking about blowing clouds away to be able to look at the stars (which was what we had been asked to do during the show at the planetarium). They had created a new game for themselves where they could revisit experiences that they had found rather frightening at the time, and try to make sense of them.

But play is not only about exploring difficult emotions or experiences. Interestingly, sometimes children create fantasy worlds that coincide directly with reality. The Russian psychologist Lev Vygotsky illustrates this with an example of two sisters, aged five and seven years, who play at being sisters. In life young children generally behave without thinking about how to behave. But in the game of sisters playing 'sisters' the young girls start to think about what it *means* to be a sister – how sisters relate to each other and how they may be seen and treated by other people. 'What passes unnoticed by the child in real life becomes a rule of behaviour in play,' Vygotsky wrote (Vygotsky 1978: 95).

Similarly, imaginary friends, who take the form of dolls or, more commonly, are invisible, can provide children with opportunities to explore difficult emotions and make sense of their world. 'In the past, having an imaginary companion was often interpreted as evidence that a child was having difficulty making real friends or was experiencing some sort of psychological distress,' says Marjorie Taylor, Professor of Psychology at the University of Oregon and author *of Imaginary Companions and the Children who Create Them*. But, she adds, 'imaginary companions are surprisingly common', and 'they play a healthy role in children's cognitive and emotional development' (Taylor January 2000). Taylor shows how having an imaginary companion can be associated with advanced social understanding – being able to take the perspective of another person.

Taylor, with Stephanie Carlson, a psychology lecturer at the University of Washington, carried out a longitudinal (long-term) study of 100 children, finding that 65 per cent of seven-year-olds have had a pretend friend at some point in their lives (Taylor *et al.* 2004). More children aged six to seven were found to have imaginary companions than children aged three to four, and some children had multiple and serial imaginary friends. 'It is somewhat of a revolving door,' said

Carlson. 'Children are nimble in coming up with these imaginary companions and sometimes we have a hard time keeping up with all of the ones a child has' (*University of Washington News* 2004). And they come in all kinds of shapes and sizes: from invisible boys and girls, squirrels, panthers and dogs to a seven-inch-tall elephant and a hundred-year-old GI Joe doll. These 'friends', the researchers claim, not only provide companionship but bear the brunt of the child's anger, provide a reference point when bargaining with parents, and can be blamed for all kinds of mishaps. The researchers argued that we should think of this as a dress rehearsal for real life, interacting with all types of characters and handling conflict resolution.

Lifting children's thinking

Children under two, before being aware of principles such as sharing and turn taking, tend mainly to engage in solitary play. In the toddler period, interactions with their peers start to become more frequent. By the end of their second year of life children spend more time in social than in solitary play. That is, they play *with* rather than just *alongside* other children, and start to reciprocate. They exchange roles, as in hide-and-seek, and turns, as in the use of toys.

In his seminal book *The Language and Thought of the Child* Piaget (2002) illustrates the role of egocentrism – that is, the inability to see the world from any perspective other than one's own – in children's thinking. Although Piaget claimed that children were fundamentally egocentric until around seven years of age, it is now widely accepted that by four years of age most children have started to comprehend that other people can have beliefs that differ from their own.

As part of the research for my Ph.D. on child development I carried out a 'Theory of Mind' test on children between three and four years of age in a primary school in Manchester. I presented the children, one of whom I shall call Mark, with a tube of Smarties. When I asked Mark what he thought was inside the tube his face lit up. 'Smarties!' he exclaimed. I handed him the tube and asked him to look inside. His face quickly fell when he realized that what was inside was *not*

Smarties after all, but crayons. I then told Mark that after he had gone back to the classroom one of his classmates, Mary, would come into the room to play the same game with me. 'I will show Mary this tube and ask her what she thinks is inside. What do you think she'll say?' Mark, like most children under four years of age, said, 'Crayons.' He knew, after having looked inside, that the tube of Smarties actually contained crayons, so of course Mary would say it contained crayons too. When I asked him what he thought was inside the tube before he opened it he again said, 'Crayons.'

Mark could not contemplate that thoughts can be different from reality. Once children are able to think about thoughts, their thinking is lifted to a different height. Piaget believed relationships between peers bring out differences of viewpoints and this helps children in developing an ability to think about thoughts or beliefs. He wrote that:

> social life is necessary if the individual is to become conscious of the functioning of his own mind ... Just as, if left to himself, the child believes every idea that enters his head instead of regarding it as a hypothesis to be verified, so the child ... believes without question everything he is told [by adults].
>
> (Piaget 1977: 388)

To a child, what adults say has a sort of mystical power, Piaget argued. Play between equals is therefore necessary in order to socialize the child – that is, to succeed in 'delivering him from the mystical power of the word of the adult' (Piaget 1977: 388).

Vygotsky also recognized the role of play in developing children's thinking. In the ground-breaking book *Mind and Society: The Development of Higher Psychological Processes*, written in the 1930s but not translated into English until 1978, Vygotsky wrote that 'In play the child always behaves beyond his average age, above his daily behaviour; in play it is as though he were a head taller than himself' (Vygotsky 1978: 102). In a certain sense, play is the leading source of development in pre-school years, Vygostky argued. Like Piaget, Vygotsky showed that imagination and make-believe play a significant role in children's development: 'Imagination is a new formation that is not present in the consciousness of the very young child, is totally absent in animals, and represents a specifically human form of conscious activity' (Vygotsky 1978: 93).

Vygotsky described children's play as both liberating and constraining. In play the child is free, but this is an illusory freedom, he wrote. Preschool children are 'free' to explore new roles in play, but, as role-playing with their peers has to be a co-operative activity, they need to exhibit an unprecedented level of self-control. Play teaches children, for the first time, to act against their impulses, as they need to subordinate themselves to the rules of the game.

Although children invent increasingly complex and fascinating make-believe situations with improvised rules, these rules need to be closely observed.

Of course, children do need to learn to behave according to certain rules from the first year of their life – but these are adult-created rules. Infants and toddlers are constantly told 'Don't touch that,' 'Don't put that in your mouth,' 'Don't throw that,' and so on. Vygotsky commented on the important insight Piaget had made in relation to the issue of rules and morality. Piaget distinguished between two distinct moralities. Some rules are imposed on children by adults. Others are made by the child himself; they are the child's own rules, as Piaget says, rules of 'self-restraint and self-determination'.

Play gives children a unique insight into rules and morals. Piaget (1977) showed in his book *Moral Judgement of the Child* that young children are dominated by a 'moral realism' – that is, they judge behaviour by its consequences rather than its intention. So, to a young child, a child who accidentally breaks a vase worth over £1,000 is 'naughtier' than a child who breaks a cheap vase while trying to steal sweets from it. Also, this 'moral realism' leads to a confusion in the child's mind between moral rules and physical rules. So, for instance, the child confuses the fact that it is physically not possible to light a match twice and the rule that they are not allowed to play with matches. But children have an entirely different attitude to rules that they make themselves. They understand that the rules are negotiable and that they are not the same as physical rules.

Also, imaginary play 'teaches the child to guide her behaviour not only by immediate perception of objects or by the situation immediately affecting her but also by the meaning of this situation', Vygotsky wrote (1978: 97). Outside of play, the behaviour of infants and toddlers is determined by the situation in which they find themselves. Their behaviour, motivations and desires are shaped by their immediate perceptions – that is, by what they see and hear at any given moment. But in imaginary play their behaviour and motives are shaped by ideas – that is, their *own* ideas – and children are for the first time able to start separating *meanings* from objects or actions.

Vygotsky showed that for young children there is 'an intimate fusion' between meanings and what is seen or heard. So, for instance, if you ask a child of two years of age to repeat the sentence 'Mummy is standing up' when their mother is in fact sitting down in front of them, the child will change the sentence to 'Mummy is sitting down'. To a young child words and objects, or words and actions, are not separate entities, but are one and the same thing. As adults, we know that 'cup' is a word for a utensil out of which one drinks. But to a young child 'cup' *is* a cup. The word *is* the object. The child cannot think about words in the abstract – as separate from the object – but can only think about the things the words represent.

However, in play a child spontaneously starts to separate meanings from objects – without knowing that he or she is doing so, it must be added. In play a cardboard box may represent a television or a piece of paper a plate. It is only when children start to learn to write that they *consciously* appreciate that there are such things as words that *represent* – but are also separate from – things. Play can therefore be seen, Vygotsky argued, as a preparatory stage in the development of children's written language.

The motivation for fantasy play

Vygotsky argued that the initial incentive for children to play comes from the 'illusory realisation of unrealisable desires' (Vygotsky 1978: 93). In other words, young children find it very difficult to cope with the restrictions the adult world puts upon them, and imaginary play provides them with a means – even if it is illusory – of realizing their desires. Play is essentially wish fulfilment, he argued.

As we entered a shop one rainy day, my husband gave me a look of absolute horror on hearing the screams of a toddler in a buggy in front of us. One could be forgiven for thinking the boy was being slowly tortured. But it was all down to him being denied the bar of chocolate he wanted. It is quite incredible what tantrums two to three-year-olds are able to throw when they do not get what they want immediately. As Vygotsky perceptively noted: 'No one has met a child under three years old who wants to do something a few days in the future' (Vygotsky, 1978: 93). Luckily young children can be distracted from what they want: and the younger the child the easier it is. But as children get older – and this is where play comes in – and cannot so easily be distracted from their immediate desires, make-believe situations serve the function of satisfying in some way those unrealized desires.

My sister-in-law tells me that her two children, aged four and two-and-a-half, are very excited about going to visit their uncle and aunt in Tunisia. But waiting several weeks to head off on their exciting adventure is too much for small children to get their heads around. So they spend a lot of time play-acting, Clare tells me, 'setting off to Tunisia in their toy cars'. To young children the adult world is full of obstacles and restrictions. Play gives them the chance to escape those restrictions.

Barriers To Young Children's Play

Having the opportunity to play is crucial for young children's development. It helps them to: control and understand emotions; satisfy their desires; develop their thinking; make sense of the adult world; and much more. And, of course, it provides pre-school children with endless fun. The report *The Importance of Play in Promoting Healthy Child Development and Maintaining Strong Parent–Child Bonds* by the American Academy of Pediatrics (AAP) states: 'When play is allowed to be child driven, children practice decision-making skills, move at their own pace, discover their own areas of interest, and ultimately engage fully in the passions they wish to pursue' (Ginsburg 2007: 183).

The increasing pressure to 'hothouse' toddlers towards academic success and give them a head start in life with more and more educational programmes, such as Baby Einstein, and tutoring for toddlers, serves no positive purpose. William Crain, professor of psychology at City College of New York, argues in *Reclaiming Childhood: Letting Children Be Children In Our Achievement-oriented Society* that adults need to provide more of an 'unobtrusive presence' so that young children can develop their own natural curiosity (Crain 2004). He is right about this. But it should be said that there is no reliable evidence that it is damaging to the young child to spend some time watching DVDs or television.

Many have argued that young children's imaginative play is being destroyed by expensive toys and new technologies – gadgets that give children no room to use their own imagination. These arguments are not convincing. There is no evidence that the way toddlers play has changed significantly in recent decades. My sister-in-law recently lamented that, after having spent a fortune on their children's Christmas presents, the children ended up spending more time playing with one of the big cardboard boxes than with any of the toys. Young children may have a multitude of toys, but they are still engaging in fantasy play with those toys – or the cartons they come in, for that matter.

What children need is sufficient freedom to make their own fantasy world and to chose how and with what they play. The number or variety of toys in their midst is not likely to restrict their play. But adults constantly butting in to direct their play may well do so.

William Kenneth Jones, narrator of *Different Times: a View of Life in Inner Manchester during the First Decades of the Twentieth Century*, describes the nature of play in the pre-1939 world as 'largely free from adult impositions and therefore its actions and choices had a large deal of latitude'. Jones points out that in any society a child needs to absorb and make sense of a whole culture – 'its language, customs, institutions, values, forms of behaviour, distortions and contradictions' – in a few short years, 'with no prior knowledge or previous experience'. Play serves an important function in aiding this process. But, Jones rightly stresses, 'play is a complex process that must be permitted to unfold in its own time and in its own way' (Jones 2006: 236).

Toy guns and political targets

The biggest barrier to children's free play today is the increasing drive to structure their activities – even in nurseries. As I outlined in Chapter 2, children's opportunities for self-directed play are being limited both in the UK and the US by the governments' excessive reliance on targets as measures of success. The 2007 American Academy of Paediatrics report on the importance of play identifies a number of factors that have contributed to the reduction in opportunities for play, but highlights the 'increased attention to academics and enrichment activities at the expense of recess or free child-centred play' (Ginsburg 2007: 182). Many school districts in the US responded to the No Child Left Behind Act of 2001, motivated by George W. Bush as a framework for bipartisan education reform, by cutting break time and the time committed to the creative arts and physical education in an effort to focus on reading and mathematics.

In the UK, from September 2008, every registered early-years provider and school is required to follow the *Early Years Foundation Stage* and monitor children's progress according to sixty-nine 'Early Learning goals'. Not content with drawing up detailed guidelines for early-years providers, with several hundred developmental milestones against which children are to be assessed, the government is providing advice on the kinds of toys children should be playing with. In a 2007 report by the Department for Children, Schools and Families (DCSF), titled *Confident, Capable and Creative: Supporting Boys' Achievements*, Ministers claim that boys' learning can be improved by their 'choices of play, particularly superhero and weapon play' (DCSF 2007c: 17).

Contrary to what was written in the UK papers about the government's 'pro-toy gun' and 'pro-superhero' play policies, this is not a case of government Ministers finally realizing that we should chill out about children's play time, and let them have fun without feeling the need to fret about their every move. Rather, the government seems to think that boys can be 'improved', and put on the right educational path, if they are pushed to partake in a bit of shoot-'em-up play time. The report claims that by encouraging boys to engage in 'weapons play' the government is putting forward a strategy for addressing 'gender differences in [educational] achievement' (DCSF 2007c: 2).

Whether or not boys, or girls for that matter, should play with toy weapons is really no concern of the government. Children have played cops 'n' robbers or cowboys 'n' indians for generations without any evidence that it leads to increased levels of aggression or criminal behaviour in later teenage and adult life. Yet nor is there any evidence that weapon play has a specific educational value, and that it can give boys the confidence and self-esteem they apparently need to compete with girls in today's educational climate. Parents and teachers should not be lectured to by the government about what are appropriate and inappropriate, or useful and non-useful, types of play.

In *Confident, Capable and Creative* Ministers try to pin the blame for the reduction in unsupervised play on teachers and parents. 'Adults can find [weapons play] particularly challenging and have a natural instinct to stop it,' the report complains (DCSF 2007c: 16). Yet if adults had a 'natural instinct' to stop fantasy aggression, then surely our parents, in earlier times, would have stopped us from playing war games and pretending to shoot, hack and blow each other up? In truth, they generally let us get on with our warmongering fantasies without butting in.

The problem lies not with mothers, fathers and teachers but rather with a culture in which we are encouraged to fret about how children relate to one another – a culture which the UK government itself, now apparently so keen on weapon play, has done a great deal to foster.

This is not good for children – and it isn't good for teachers and parents, either. In his book *Worried all the Time* the American psychotherapist David Anderegg provides some interesting insights into the damage that constant fretting can do, especially to the well-being of parents themselves. By 'overthinking and overworrying', parents are 'eventually overacting on the decision arrived at in a worried state', says Anderegg (2003: 4). Anderegg says he is regularly approached by anxious parents who have tied themselves in knots over rather mundane questions relating to their children – the kind of things that our parents never really worried about. According to Anderegg, the problem with constantly worrying about issues such as whether children should be allowed to play with toy guns is that 'the choices multiply into an infinitude of decisions that seem like they might determine the course of our children's lives' (Anderegg 2003: 4).

If parents and teachers feel compelled to consider whether children should be allowed to play with toy guns, what stance would they take on children holding up their thumbs and index fingers and shouting 'Bang, bang'? Should that also be stopped? What about water pistols? Paint-balling? But then, what if the child who is denied the opportunity to go on a paint-ball outing ends up being ostracized by his peers? Once 'overworrying' is institutionalized the list of potential problems facing children goes on and on.

It is sad that parents and teachers are encouraged to waste so much of their mental energy on issues which, when push comes to shove, really do not matter very much. Whether or not children should be allowed to bring toy weapons to school should be up to the school itself. There may be good reasons for not allowing replica guns in playgrounds. But schools should not be restricting children's unsupervised play. They should not be preventing play-fighting or rough-and-tumble play, whether it involves chasing, wrestling, kicking or feigned attacks. This type of play helps children form and maintain friendships, and it is important for the development of their social competence.

Friendship, intimacy and privacy

The Children's Society's 2007 Good Childhood Inquiry points out that play is essential for children and young people because it allows them to practise forming and consolidating friendships and dealing with conflict.

Our relationships with friends are very different from those with parents and siblings. Unlike family relationships, particularly adult–child relationships, peer relationships are based on a degree of equality between the participants. This allows more negotiation of the terms of the relationship. Also, unlike family relations, which one cannot pick and choose, peer relationships can be relatively easily established and just as easily destroyed. Our parents and siblings are generally stuck with us whether they or we like it or not. But there is always the danger that friends, if we say or do something that hurts or annoys them, will declare, 'I'm not your friend any more.' Children therefore need to make much more of an effort to consolidate and maintain relationships with their peers than with their siblings and parents – or any other adult, for that matter.

In *Recess: Its Role in Education and Development* Minnesota-based educationalist Anthony Pellegrini argues that friendships require a high level of sophistication – such as being able to co-operate, compromise and inhibit aggression. Because children enjoy interacting with their peers they have a vested interest in learning such difficult and demanding strategies: 'This combination of high levels of sophistication necessary to interact with peers and high motivation means that peer-interaction contexts are powerful venues for skill learning and development' (Pellegrini 2005: 38).

When I went to pick up my niece Maja, then aged four, from nursery during a visit to Norway, and asked her if I could meet her best friend, Irene, I was sulkily told 'No,' because they were *uvenner* (Norwegian for 'not friends'). Apparently Irene had thrown two stones at Maja, and when Maja picked up a stone to throw back, Irene declared that she no longer wanted to be her friend. Of course Maja thought the whole episode was very unfair, as she hadn't even thrown a stone. Yet by the time I had finished my ten-minute tour of the nursery Irene had given Maja a bouquet of dandelions and they were best friends again. As her nursery teacher told me, they frequently fall out, but they always make up again.

Children will often end up in disputes with their friends – disputes that can be a lot more upsetting than the tiff between Maja and Irene. But through conflict and argument they gain a better understanding of what they can expect from each other and start to learn how to make amends and resolve conflicts. The formation of childhood friendships will inevitably involve intimacy and trust, as well as tension and conflict. Research has shown that with young children there is often *more* conflict between friends than between peers in general. This could be a result of them setting higher expectations of the behaviour of their friends than of other children. Also, they use friendships to test boundaries and explore what is appropriate and acceptable behaviour.

As children grow up friendships become increasingly important to their social and emotional development, as well as their general well-being. A study by the British Social Issues Research Centre (SIRC) found that young men and women value friendships very highly. They invest time, commitment and emotion in their friends, and expect the same in return. Respondents emphasized trust and loyalty, always 'being there' for each other, and 'being oneself' as the principal and most vital elements of friendship (SIRC 2007).

The Children's Society's Good Childhood Inquiry found that in response to the question 'If you need help with a problem, who is the person you are most likely to talk to?' children were most likely to go to their friends (46 per cent), followed by a parent (35 per cent). The report concluded, 'Having friends helps children to develop a sense of identity and social belonging and to learn a sense of "everyday morality" in the way they treat others' (Children's Society 2007: 5).

American psychologist Thomas Berndt has for many years been investigating the role of friendships, particularly in adolescence. He challenges the prevailing myth, in both popular and academic debates, that 'peer pressure' has a negative effect on today's youth. 'A social function of friendships is to give adolescents a sense of belonging in the social world and allies in navigating through the world,' he writes (Berndt 1999: 51). Interactions with friends also play a central role in identity formation – that is, helping teenagers to define who they are.

Friends have a significant influence on adolescents, on everything from how hard they work at school to what music they listen to. Of course, that influence can be for good or ill, but research suggests that it is more likely to be positive than negative. For instance, more adolescents report that their friends discourage rather than encourage smoking and drinking. And most adolescents report that their friends encourage them to study for tests and try for higher grades (Berndt 1999).

Lack of unsupervised play could reduce children's opportunities to form deep and lasting friendships. Evidence from *The Good Childhood Inquiry* suggests that the number of teenagers who have no best friend has risen from one in eight twenty years ago to one in five in 2007. The author of one of the submissions to the inquiry argued that, considering the importance of friendship to children, maybe there should be a re-evaluation of the purpose of education and teacher training in terms of 'the ability to promote co-operation and friendship between students'.

The lack of best friends is clearly a problem – but to suggest it can be solved by anyone other than the children themselves misses the point. Children cannot be taught, in the abstract, about how to make friends. It is through unsupervised play – through conflict and co-operation – that children are given the opportunity to develop friendships and to build up relationships of trust. The key is therefore to ensure children are given time and space with their peers, away from adult supervision. In Chapter 6 I explore how society's obsession with bullying has led to a raft of behavioural codes that now regulate playground behaviour, and the increasingly interventionist role of adults in children's disputes, which could be limiting children's opportunities to form lasting friendships.

'When the contemporary childhood experience is one of containment and surveillance, what becomes of self-discovery and self-realisation?' asks Libby Brooks in *The Story of Childhood: Growing up in Modern Britain*. 'Without privacy, both physical and psychological, how do children become aware of their deepest needs and impulses?' (Brooks 2006: 45). These are important questions. Privacy, a space for reflection, experimentation and discovery, is as necessary for children as it is for adults. As John Fitzpatrick, Director of Kent Law Clinic, has written on *spiked*, private space is key to allowing individuals to 'think and fantasize and experiment and plan [and behave] unconstrained by fear of recrimination or censure or exposure' (Fitzpatrick May 2007). Privacy is central to the process of deciding who we are and how we want to present ourselves to the world, Fitzpatrick explains.

The need for adult guidance

Insightful US commentators have argued that the key driving force in the excessive timetabling of children's activities is an obsession with achievement and a desire to protect children from every conceivable failure or disappointment. This apprehension about children's future success has resulted in what US psychologist David Elkind calls 'hyper-parenting', where children's free time is over-programmed and over-regulated (Elkind 2001). Children are ferried around from one extracurricular activity to another. US educationalist Chris Mercogliano similarly writes:

> 'Helicopter parents' can be found hovering protectively over their offspring, ready to swoop in and rescue them at the first sign of trouble. ... They pave their way, fight their battles for them, and generally deny them free rein to succeed or fail on their own.
>
> (Mercogliano 2007: 5)

There is definitely some truth in this. As journalist Jennie Bristow points out in her 'guide to subversive parenting' on *spiked*:

> The widespread notion that parents and parenting determine every-thing about a child's behaviour and well-being, from their weight to their literacy levels to their general happiness and the number of GCSEs/ASBOs they may receive, has led to a situation where parents are more likely to live their own lives through their children.
>
> (Bristow 29 August 2007)

The flip side of this, as Bristow points out, is that children end up blaming their parents for everything that goes wrong.

Unfortunately many recent books unhelpfully counterpoise the value of play to the regimented nature of schooling, in particular testing. Vygotsky gives us a different take on this issue. He developed the concept of the Zone of Proximal Development (ZPD) to illustrate how children learn and develop. This is a concept that has become hugely popular in education circles, but which is often stripped of its core meaning. It is frequently used to bolster the rather fashionable idea of 'child-centred learning', which boils down to the view that children should not be given too many challenges. But this goes against the spirit of the ZPD, which Vygotsky defined as 'the distance between the actual developmental level as determined by independent problem solving and the level of potential development as determined through problem solving under adult guidance, or in collaboration with more capable peers' (Vygotsky, 1978: 86).

In other words, the basis for development is being forced to adopt new strategies and behaviours because existing forms of thought are not adequate for the particular task. Play can create such a ZPD for the child, according to Vygotsky, but so too can formal education.

Adults can, through instruction and guidance, propel children beyond what they are capable of in the here and now. Play is important, but so are adult-directed teaching and learning. The new target-driven approach to education on both sides of the Atlantic is indeed anathema to creative teaching, but that does not mean that academics and testing *per se* are problems. A good teacher, according to Vygotsky, should expect more of the child than it is capable of today without adult guidance. At the core of the concept of ZPD is the need to provide children with constant challenges, but challenges that are manageable.

Today's obsession with protecting children from failure, and attempt to mould them to a predetermined shape, are not healthy. Children cannot be manufactured like an artefact, or trained like a dog. To become fully rounded human beings, children need to be given the space to develop their own identity, and to be given the opportunity to make decisions, to recognize their own needs, interests and desires, and to form their own dreams and aspirations – all of which are central to becoming an autonomous adult. Play, friendship and privacy are key components of this process.

But giving children the space they need to develop does not mean denying the impact that adult guidance has upon them. Children's outlook and aspirations will be influenced and shaped by the adults in their midst – either through the aspiration to be like them, or as a reaction against adults and what they stand for.

SIX

THE BULLYING BANDWAGON

Despite anxieties about stranger danger and unsafe streets, it's children's peers from whom they require most protection, in the relentlessly familiar environment of the playground. We ask of children what few adults would tolerate: to endure hours of enforced proximity to their tormentors.

(Libby Brooks, 2006, p. 198)

While some voices in recent years have spoken up to challenge the safety-first culture surrounding children today, drawing attention to the problem of raising a generation of cosseted, 'cotton wool' kids and arguing the need for children to be able to take more physical risks, one rarely hears any objection to the notion that children increasingly need to be protected from the 'emotional risks' posed to them by their peers in the form of bullying.

In this respect the old adage 'Sticks and stones may break my bones / But words will never hurt me' has been turned on its head. Some may concede that kids today could do with a few more broken bones, if this allows them the freedom to climb trees or play conkers; but the notion that children can be damaged for life as a result of insults hurled at them by their fellow pupils has become accepted as common sense. Consequently, the raft of behavioural codes that now regulate playground behaviour, and the increasingly interventionist role of adults in children's disputes, is seen as a necessary and humane development.

But the anti-bullying crusade has its own problems. The most serious is that children's relationships with other children are assumed to be damaging, and children are tacitly encouraged to look upon their peers with trepidation and suspicion. As more and more forms of behaviour are labelled as 'bullying' more and more children become labelled as 'bullies' or 'victims'.

Today children are pushed to look upon their everyday encounters with their friends or enemies through the prism of potential violence and abuse, and encouraged to seek help from teachers or other adults. This leads to a situation where children can become unwilling to, and incapable of, resolving their own problems with their peers: a process that damages children's development, and their relationships with each other, far more than the odd stone thrown or insult shouted.

Bullying in perspective

For a minority of children, bullying is a profound problem. Each year we read tragic news stories of children taking their own lives after years of incessant bullying. In 2004 thirteen-year-old Laura Rhodes from Neath, South Wales, took a fatal overdose. Her parents said she had been terrified by the bullying and taunts she endured each day. The same year, twelve-year-old Aaron Armstrong was found hanged in a hayshed at the family farm in County Antrim in Ireland after being bullied at school.

In the 2007 book *Bullycide in America* a number of mothers tell the most painful stories of their lives – having watched their loved ones suffer and struggle because of bullying and eventually seeing no other way out but to end their short lives (High 2007). The book is edited by Brenda High, who lost her thirteen-year-old son, Jared, to suicide in September 1998.

Such stories are heart-breaking: and that is why we need to put the discussion about bullying in its proper perspective. Much that is defined as bullying today is not bullying. It is boisterous banter or everyday playground disputes that could – and should – be resolved *without* adult intervention. Treating all playground disputes as serious acts of abuse does not help victims of terrible bullying, like Laura, Aaron and Jared. In fact it discourages a proper sense of vigilance about real brutality perpetrated by a handful of children, in favour of problematizing all relationships between all children.

Parents are continually warned by governments, teachers' unions, charities and the media about the effect of bullying on children's well-being. The UK government's Department for Children, Schools and Families (DCSF) makes a big deal out of its commitment to dealing with school bullies. From September 1999 head teachers have been under a duty to 'draw up measures to prevent all forms of bullying among pupils'. The DCSF web site states:

> We attach a high priority to helping schools prevent and combat bullying: it is a serious problem which puts the emotional well-being and educational achievement of pupils at risk. All schools should treat bullying seriously and take steps to combat it promptly and firmly whenever and wherever it occurs.

The government document *Building Brighter Futures*, outlining its ten-year Children's Plan, states: 'Bullying can destroy lives and have immeasurable impact on young people's confidence, self-esteem, mental health and social and emotional development' (DCSF 2007a: 48).

There is no shortage of studies showing that bullying is considered to be a big problem about which something should be done – and these are always cited to back up proposals to intensify anti-bullying measures in schools. For example, a survey funded by the National Institute of Child Health and Human Development (NICHD) has led to claims that bullying is widespread in American schools, with more than 16 per cent of US schoolchildren saying they were bullied by other students during the current term (Nansel *et al.* 2001). Surveys conducted in the UK have found far higher rates of bullying, but this may be the result of the research being less rigorous. The Thomas

Coram Research Unit found that over half of British primary (51 per cent) and secondary school pupils (54 per cent) thought that bullying was 'a big problem' or 'quite a problem' in their school (Oliver and Candappa 2003). Just over half (51 per cent) of pupils in Year 5 reported that they themselves had been bullied during the last term. Of the pupils in Year 8 the figure was a lot lower: just over a quarter (28 per cent) said that they had been bullied that term.

More worryingly, the 2006 National Bullying Survey carried out by BullyingUK found that 69 per cent of almost 5,000 children surveyed had been bullied, with 33 per cent of parents expressing fear that their child might be suicidal because of bullying. As the Anti-Bullying Alliance (ABA) boasts, 'The survey was widely publicised on national TV, radio and in newspapers as well as in young people's magazines and on youth, charity, police and council websites' (ABA 2006). It should be noted that this was an internet survey. The high proportion of children claiming to have been bullied may be explained by those children being bullied being more likely to take part in such a survey – a classic problem with self-reported surveys.

We need to ask ourselves what all these disturbingly high figures actually mean. The problem with claims that bullying is on the rise, or that half or more of all schoolchildren are the victims of bullying, is that bullying is today defined as anything slightly unpleasant. On its web site the counselling hot line ChildLine describes bullying as: 'being called names; being teased; being pushed or pulled about; being hit or attacked; having money and other possessions taken or messed about with; having rumours spread about you; being ignored and left out', and the list goes on.

Norwegian psychologist Dan Olweus has been an influential figure internationally, over the last two decades, in the shift that has taken place, from viewing bullying as a normal, though unfortunate, part of school and everyday life to a pressing social issue that needs to be addressed. Not so very long ago bullying was perceived as a nasty rite of passage that a lot of people went through and got over. From Tom Brown being roasted over an open fire by a bully in Thomas Hughes's classic nineteenth-century novel to the many accounts, in the genre of boarding-school novels that *Tom Brown's Schooldays* spawned, of the brutality meted out when 'fagging' for prefects (beatings, heads pushed down toilets, and so on), it is clear that the existence of bullying is not new. What has changed is the emphasis today on the emotional aspect of bullying rather than the physical harm that it can cause. Olweus, therefore, defines bullying as 'Intentional, repeated hurtful acts, words, or other behaviour, such as name-calling, threatening and/or shunning committed by one or more children against another'. Note how even in this comparatively rigorous definition, no distinction is made between physical attacks ('sticks and stones') and emotional jibes ('words'). Similarly the researcher who conducted the NICHD survey in the US defined bullying as 'a specific type of aggression in which the behaviour is intended to harm or disturb, [occurs] repeatedly over time, and there is an imbalance of power, with a more powerful person or group attacking a less powerful one' (Nansel *et al.* 2001: 2094).

Given the emphasis on the verbal/emotional aspect of bullying today, it is not surprising that recent years have brought increasing concern about what goes on outside the school gates – even between children separated by a physical distance of several miles. The US Department for Homeland Security warns on its Computer Emergency Readiness Team web site that:

> Bullies are now taking advantage of technology to intimidate and harass their victims ... Forms of cyberbullying can range in severity from cruel or embarrassing rumours to threats, harassment, or stalking. It can affect any age group; however, teenagers and young adults are common victims, and cyberbullying is a growing problem in schools.
>
> (www.us-cert.gov/cas/tips/ST06–005.html)

The UK's DCFS web site 'Don't suffer in silence' presents the problem of 'cyberbullying' as follows:

> The advent of cyberbullying adds a new and worrying dimension to the problem of bullying – there's no safe haven for the person

being bullied. Unlike other forms of bullying, cyberbullying can follow children and young people into their private spaces and outside school hours. Cyberbullies can communicate their messages to a wide audience with remarkable speed, and can often remain unidentifiable and unseen.

(DCSF 2008)

The web site flags up seven categories of cyberbullying: text message bullying; picture/video clip bullying via mobile phone cameras; phone call bullying via mobile phone; e-mail bullying; chat room bullying; bullying through text messaging; bullying via web sites.

According to the children's charity Beat Bullying we face an 'epidemic' of mobile phone bullying. John Carr, technology adviser for children's charity NCH, said:

We know from our everyday work that any type of bullying can be a nightmare for children and young people. As technology has become more sophisticated, so has the way children are bullied. One in five have [*sic*] been bullied by mobile phone or computer and for many there is no escape.

(BBC Online 25 July 2006)

In July 2007 schools Minister Jim Knight announced that the government would ask technology firms to help in the fight against bullying:

No child should suffer the misery of bullying, on line or off line, and we will support schools in tackling it in cyberspace with the same vigilance as in the playground ... The education Bill will give teachers a legal right to discipline pupils, strengthening their authority to take firm action on bullying. It will also send a strong message to parents and pupils that bullying will not be tolerated, with court-imposed parenting orders to compel parents of bullies to attend parenting classes or face £1,000 fines.

(BBC Online 25 July 2006)

The Professional Association of Teachers welcomed the new guidance (BBC Online 25 July 2006).

Given the ubiquitous use of technologies such as mobile phones and the internet by young people, and the intimacy of the relationship between children and their mobile phones or message boards, it is easy to understand how children can, indeed, become as deeply upset by an abusive text message as they can by an anonymous note or an unpleasant spate of name calling. But with the exception of 'happy slapping', where a physical attack happens first, 'cyberbullying' is about as far away from a fire-roasting, toilet-shoving bully tactic as it is possible to get. Put bluntly, if bullying can be defined as meaning anything that takes place anywhere – even between two children on different continents – doesn't it cease to mean anything at all?

The more broadly bullying is defined the more children could be described as being bullied. Someone having fun at someone else's expense, or being shunned by a group of friends, cannot feature too infrequently in most children's everyday lives. I am sure that my experience of at times being left out of certain friendship circles at school is not that uncommon – though I didn't define it as bullying then, and I wouldn't now. My family moved from Bergen to Trondheim when I was nine years of age and my siblings and I all went through the mortifying experience of being laughed at by other schoolkids because of our Bergen accent (which is quite unique, but charming, in my biased view). We all battled to get rid of our accents as quickly as possible. But although it was upsetting and frightening suddenly to be treated as an outsider, many of the same children later became good friends of ours.

Some childhood experiences are hurtful, and when you are a child a nasty taunt or a falling-out with your best friend genuinely does seem like the end of the world. That is very different, though, from the experience being harmful. Being left out of a playground game may make a child cry for a week, but by the following week it is likely to be involved again and all is forgotten. Children are not emotionally scarred by the experience; they get over it and move on. Once the experience is labelled as 'bullying', however, and a teacher becomes involved, it becomes an issue of much greater significance, driving a more permanent wedge between the putative victim and that week's bullies, and making it far harder for the spontaneous dynamics of playground life to resolve themselves.

The thrust of anti-bullying campaigns is to push teachers or other authority figures into children's conflicts on an everyday basis, in order to prevent 'bullying'. Such campaigns also push the message to children about the importance of telling somebody (i.e. a teacher, parent or other adult) if they are worried about bullying, either for their own sake or on behalf of a friend. But when bullying comes to mean anything that happens anywhere, this emphasis on involving a third (adult) party in a children's conflict is highly problematic. Throughout over a century of children's fiction, telling tales and running to teacher have stood as beacons of guidance about What Not To Do in terms of winning the respect of your peers and teaching bullies a lesson. Whether standing up to bullies involves a physical fight-back or another, cleverer strategy is immaterial. The point is that is has been well understood that what counts, above all, is children's ability to manage conflict themselves; after which point the conflict usually becomes resolved. If teachers become involved in every playground spat or squabble, it both blows the incident out of proportion and undermines the child's ability to manage the situation.

When the official concern with bullying extends outside the school gates to children's free time in the offline and online world, the dynamic towards adult intervention becomes even more of a concern. Cyberspace is not policed by teachers or counsellors – that is one of the key reasons why children love it. Cyberbullying is an unavoidable consequence of having the technology available that enables children to communicate freely with others across a vast physical space, and children's desire to use and explore that technology free from the constraints that exist in the 'real world' of teachers and parents. If children are to be allowed that opportunity, they will also have to deal with one of the consequences: a cyberspace with no bullies in it would not be a cyberspace they would want to visit. It seems a shame that the frantic desire to protect children from the consequences of name calling is

threatening one of the few arenas they have left to develop and conduct relationships with each other outside the increasingly small, closely
monitored worlds of home and school.

Dealing with bullying

There is a further danger with the notion that bullying can be anything,
happening anywhere. If teachers are encouraged to see bullying in every
childhood argument, they can easily lose the ability to see the wood
for the trees. Truly debilitating bullying is thankfully rare, and this
does need to be dealt with by adults, in a firm but sensitive manner.
Yet if adults are encouraged to see just about any negative behaviour
as bullying and to take action immediately, they could end up failing
to act when a serious problem is staring them in the face.

Take the case of Benjamin Cox. In May 2007 a Supreme Court judge
in Australia awarded eighteen-year-old Benjamin Cox A$220,000, to be
paid by the New South Wales Department of Education, for the pain
and suffering he experienced as a result of being bullied. He was awarded a substantial additional sum for the economic loss that his trauma
would cause him. Justice Carolyn Simpson said, 'He will never know the
satisfaction of employment. He will suffer anxiety and depression for
the rest of his life. He is unlikely to form any relationships. He has no
friends and is unlikely to make any' (News.com.au 15 May 2007).

Benjamin undoubtedly suffered at the hands of some rather nasty
children. One incident – where a child had allegedly tried to strangle
him – left him unconscious. Several months later he lost a tooth after
the same child tried to ram his school jumper down his throat. Most
parents would, quite understandably, be distraught if their child
should face such a level of intimidation, knowing the fear and emotional pain that go with it, let alone the physical dangers. There are
times when teachers clearly need to step in to reprimand children who
are overstepping the mark, and in this case the school should surely
have done something a lot earlier.

Yet, even here, there is something worrying about Justice Simpson's
statement that Benjamin will be damaged by the experience until the

end of his days. Can it be right to tell an eighteen-year-old boy that his life is effectively over – that he 'will suffer anxiety and depression for the rest of his life' and 'is unlikely to form any relationships'? If adults talk about bullying as an experience that will blight the entire rest of their lives, children are less likely to find strategies to cope with and get over hurtful incidences. Although anti-bullying campaigns may have emerged out of concern for children's emotional welfare, they could end up projecting their own fears and insecurities on to children, and in the process making things worse.

The way children interpret events, and the emotional mark that these events leave on them, are very much shaped by the way adults respond to the events. Studies looking at the effect of early traumatic experiences on children's emotional development have found that neither the severity of the event nor the age of the child at the time can help us predict whether the child will experience behavioural or emotional problems later on. As child development expert Rudolph Schaffer points out:

> It has become apparent that there is no direct relationship between age and the impact [of] experience on the individual, that young children are not necessarily more vulnerable even to quite severe adversities than older children, and that considerable variability exists in long-term outcome.
>
> (Schaffer 2000: 5)

The one variable that does seem to help predict the impact of traumatic events on later development is how the adults cope with the situation. If an adult breaks down and seems unable to comprehend what is going on, it is likely to have a detrimental impact on the children in his or her care.

So if the message to children who are being bullied is 'When bad things happen to you, your life could be destroyed for ever' could this response not be more damaging to children in the long term than the bullying itself? If we treat children as if they could not possibly cope with hurtful experiences, we are more likely to undermine their confidence and make them less likely to cope with difficult events in the future.

Little adults?

Part of the confusion surrounding today's obsession with bullying is that children's behaviour towards one another – the words they use, the bluntness of their actions in, say, excluding one another from playground games – is viewed with the same seriousness as it would be if adults were employing that kind of behaviour towards one another.

In an article in the *Times Education Supplement* Stuart Waiton, Director of Generation Youth Issues in Scotland, describes getting his first official letter about his seven-year-old son's bullying antics at school. 'It turned out to be based largely on his teasing a neighbour's son for playing with my daughter "up a tree, K I S S I N G." In the end, the school realized that the incident was not important and it was resolved' (Waiton 27 July 2007). Waiton voices concern about today's inability to treat kids as kids. 'After all, if children were just mini-adults, there would be no teasing about kissing, although there may be some questions raised about why this was being done up a tree,' he writes (Waiton 27 July 2007).

Whereas in the past it was accepted that children, in their unsophistication, would employ the kind of tactless, heartless, even in-your-face offensive behaviour that adults could not get away with, today such behaviour in the playground is seen as just as shocking and problematic as if it were between adults in an office.

One example is the growing concern with 'racist behaviour' among young children. Adrian Hart, a community video maker in east London, told me that he became concerned about today's anti-bullying and anti-racist policies when working on a government-funded educational film about racism in schools. Teachers in the UK are today obliged under the Race Relations (Amendment) Act 2000 to record officially the number of racist incidents in their school. TeacherNet, a government-supported education resource, defines a racist incident as 'any incident which is perceived to be racist by the victim or any other person'. This definition is in line with the 1999 Macpherson report, the landmark inquiry into the police investigation of the murder of black teenager Stephen Lawrence in 1993, which famously accused the police of 'institutional racism' and laid the basis for the framework for official anti-racist policies in Britain subsequently. This has, Hart tells me, 'generated an army of race-equality officials and a raft of "interventions" – awareness-raising drama workshops, special assemblies, books, videos and teaching packs'.

As more and more teachers are looking for racist incidents, the statistics show that racism among children is on the rise. The most recent figures available from the DCSF show a 29 per cent rise over one year in the number of pupils suspended from school for racist abuse (Meikle 13 April 2007). Sarah Teather, education spokesman for the Liberal Democrats, who obtained the figures through parliamentary questions, said, '[This is] another shocking picture of the poor state of race relations in Britain today' (Meikle 13 April 2007). The Commission for Racial Equality said it 'hints that [racism] is deep-rooted and ingrained' (Meikle 14 April 2007). But does it, really?

In 2006 a ten-year-old boy in Manchester, England, was charged with a racially aggravated public order offence for calling another school boy a 'Paki'. District Judge Jonathan Finestein described the decision to prosecute a primary school boy as 'crazy' and 'political correctness gone mad'. He said when he was at school he was repeatedly called 'fat', but in those days the headmaster would have just given the children a 'good clouting', asked them to shake hands, and sent them on their way. During the preliminary hearing the court was told the boys are now friends and play football together.

Thankfully it is still very rare for the Crown Prosecution Service to take up cases of racist abuse in schools.

Hart believes today's view of childhood is 'as an experience teetering on the brink of a *Lord of the Flies* meltdown'. He told me, 'A view of society as in a state of perpetual malaise, of humans as either self-seeking bullies or downtrodden victims and schools as centres for correction and therapy, is a view alive and well amongst my colleagues.' At one of the schools Hart visited he asked a teacher whether everyday playground spats are being elevated, somewhat erroneously, into racist incidents. 'He looked horrified,' said Hart, 'so I attempted to clarify. "Surely when kids fall out they grab anything that will hurt, then minutes later they're friends again?" "We have to be seen to be taking racism seriously," the teacher answered. "It's the law.'"

Some teachers, however, are alarmed by the effect of this official anti-racism on relationships between their pupils. One head teacher told Hart:

> I think we're a good school, but because we are trying to be responsible and abide by the policy on racist incidents, our problem is that it's having the opposite effect. In fact it's creating an absolutely awful atmosphere around the school. Children who used to play beautifully together are starting to separate along racial lines.

By viewing childish insults through the prism of adult politics, racial divisions are simply assumed to exist. But just as a seven-year-old calling somebody 'Fatso', for example, should not be taken as seriously as if a thirty-year-old used that insult, what children mean by calling somebody a 'Paki' is not the same as an adult using the word. And by attempting to deal with such insults by elevating them into racist incidents, racial divisions are actively created: as children are made aware of the penalty of drawing attention to any apparent racial differences, it is hardly surprising that they might play safe by sticking to their own ethnic group.

We need to appreciate that kids are kids. But today they are instead portrayed either as nasty little brutes or as helpless victims. It is true that children argue. They trade insults. They fight. But, more often than not, they make up again.

It seems like the world is suffering from some form of collective amnesia – talking about kids punching and kicking each other while being encouraged by onlookers as evidence of the degeneration of society and the barbarity of today's youth. Yet I remember at primary school in Norway, whenever a fight broke out in the playground, kids would gather round shouting, 'Mere blod, mere blod,' 'More blood, more blood,' until teachers came and broke it up. In Britain the tradition of children from one school going, *en masse*, at the end of the day to witness a fight between some of their fellow pupils and kids from a neighbouring school – and to cheer their side on – is well known. A relative of mine has told me a few stories about what went on in the school playgrounds in the 1940s when he was a young boy, where a clear pecking order was established among the boys on the basis of 'how good you were with your fists'.

My friend Elsie recently stunned my nephews by recounting a story about her brother becoming the 'cock of his school' back in the 1930s. (It took them a while to realize that the word had a different meaning in the past.) Elsie's brother and a fellow pupil had been getting into a lot of fights, and quite a bit of trouble, at school. The headmaster decided to sort things out once and for all by arranging for all the pupils to gather in the school playground at the end of the school day. He set up a fight between Elsie's brother and the other boy, letting them pummel each other until he felt he could identify a clear winner. After a few rounds he eventually prised them apart, raised Elsie's brother's hand in the air and announced him to be the winner. 'They never fought after that,' Elsie said, 'and my brother at that moment became the cock of the school.' Nobody messed with him, and he didn't get into any more fights.

In *The People in the Playground*, a fascinating book describing primary school children's play that is based on regular visits to a school playground between January 1970 and November 1983, Iona Opie, world-renowned folklorist and researcher on children's 'street culture', writes:

> Fights add to the excitement of the playground, and a fight can be a main, if not the only, event of a morning playtime. Two boys sufficiently angry with each other to start an impromptu boxing match may draw a huge crowd, layers deep in a circle. The cheering eventually attracts the notice of a teacher, who comes and breaks up the contest.
>
> (Opie 1993: 10)

Iona Opie explains that if a crowd doesn't gather the fight can go on and on. In an observation on 17 February 1971 she wrote:

After the bell had gone two boys remained. They were unaware of anyone else or of themselves. Their only thought was murder; they were belting each other as hard as they could. A girl who was standing beside me said placidly, 'They *are* in a mood, aren't they!'

Opie 1993: 10)

'But girls fight, too,' adds Opie. 'Not so frequently, and in a more feminine way, with much screaming and pulling of hair' (Opie 1993: 10).

Indeed, when *The Lore and Language of Schoolchildren*, written by Iona Opie and her husband Peter, was first published in 1959 it took many adults by surprise. 'They were astonished and horrified that children possessed such an extensive underworld culture of their own and were – as [one commentator] put it – "all little savages",' Iona Opie recounts in *The People in the Playground* (Opie 1993: 12). When children's behaviour is put under the microscope to the extent that it is today they may well come across as little savages, and, more often than not, as rather stupid. But, as Opie explains, 'Children are making first encounters in words and first experiments in the physical world' (Opie 1993: 12). Preventing them from doing this does children no good, in the short or long term.

Why kids need playgrounds

In an extreme example of how the desire to protect children from bullying can prevent them from forming relationships altogether, the state school Thomas Deacon city academy in Peterborough, Cambridgeshire, proposed that it should not build a playground. Staff insisted that this would help protect pupils falling victim to playground bullies. Miles Delap, project manager at the academy, said: 'For a school of this size, a playground would have had to be huge. That would have been almost uncontrollable. We have taken away an uncontrollable space to prevent bullying and truancy' (Beckford 8 May 2007).

Many media commentators in the UK responded with derision. Libby Purves, columnist for the *Times* (London), noted, 'We newsmongers make sterling efforts to entertain, but it is not often that the reader can gasp with disbelief, snort with outrage and then collapse in hysterical giggles' (Purves 8 May 2007). But that was precisely her response, she claimed, to a school being built without a playground. Parents were also up in arms about this nonsensical decision.

In fact a school without an 'uncontrollable' playground is the logical conclusion of the current obsession with trying to create a bully-free culture. In Britain, because of fears about bullying, there is increasing hostility to school break time. Psychologists Antony Pellegrini and Peter Blatchford found that in just five years between 1990 to 1995 the lunchtime break in English schools had been reduced by 38 per cent in junior and secondary schools and 26 per cent in primary schools (Pellegrini and Blatchford 2000). The main reason given by school staff for the decrease in break time was to increase time spent on meeting the requirements of the National Curriculum. A second reason was to reduce behavioural problems, such as bullying.

A similar trend can be identified in the US, where many schools have already been built without playgrounds. According to Rhonda Clements, President of the American Association of the Child's Right to Play, an estimated 40 per cent of US school districts have eliminated break time or are considering eliminating it (Clements 2004). Some school districts give 'safety and supervision' as the reasons for getting rid of break time, explained Clements. But break time is also eliminated by many school districts in order to expand the curriculum. At the same time, the growth of the 'bedroom culture' among children means that there has been a dramatic reduction in the opportunities for peer interactions outside school.

This is a worrying trend. Children need free time to play, have fun, stumble into difficulties and work out how to resolve differences. By focusing on bullying we can end up denying children the experiences they need to develop. Break time is an important context for children to learn how to make decisions, take turns, and consolidate or break off friendships – and, of course, to let off steam and have some fun.

Iona Opie writes in the *People in the Playground*:

> Try to analyse the sound of children at play: the thin screaming
> noise can be heard from several streets away. Vitality? Yes. But
> come closer and step into the playground: a kind of defiant light-
> heartedness envelops you. The children are clowning. They are
> making fun of life; and if any enquiring adult become too serious
> about words and rules they say: 'It's only a game, isn't it? It's just
> for fun. *I* don't know what it means. It doesn't *matter*.'
>
> (Opie 1993: 15)

US sociologist William Corsaro shows that conflict, especially arguments and teasing, can 'help bring children together and help organize
activities':

> Recent research on peer conflict among elementary school chil-
> dren shows how disputes are a basic means for construction of
> social order, cultivating, testing and maintaining friendships,
> and developing and displaying social identity ... Disputes, teasing
> and conflict can add a creative tension that increases [play's]
> enjoyment.
>
> (Corsaro, 1999: 34)

To adults it may not look much like fun. Tim Gill, writer and consultant on childhood and former Director of the UK Children's Play
Council, astutely points out that much of what looks to adults like
bad behaviour is simply children practising and getting the hang of all
social and emotional skills. Whether it be expressing feelings and
recognizing the feelings of others, understanding what counts as acceptable and unacceptable in different groups and contexts, or knowing
the difference between mock anger and real anger – children can learn
these skills, Gill says, only 'if they are given the chance to practise them.
A lot' (Gill 2006: 5). Children need to learn the consequences of being
rude, and learn how to undo the potential damage to a friendship
caused by having hurt that friend.

Michael Boulton, Senior Lecturer in Psychology at the University of Chester, has shown, through hours of research, that adults can easily overestimate the extent of unacceptable behaviour in the playground, confusing rough-and-tumble play for aggression (Boulton 1994, 1992; Boulton and Smith 1990). Though superficially similar, rough-and-tumble play – which may involve chasing, wrestling, kicking, play-fighting and feigned attacks – is generally non-aggressive and tends to take place between friends. This type of play helps children to form and maintain friendships and, according to Boulton, is particularly important for the development of social competence in boys. Extensive research has shown that rough-and-tumble play helps children learn to regulate and interpret emotions. This means that when adults worry about bullying and intervene in children's arguments or fights, it could interfere with an important developmental function.

Similarly, an Institute of Education study found that teasing should not necessarily be conflated with bullying (Blatchford 1999). The study showed that teasing is widespread in interactions between school pupils. Pupils often emphasized that teasing was not something they saw as harmful, but as a part of everyday banter, often between friends. According to the developmental psychologist Peter Blatchford:

> Some teasing no doubt serves a social purpose, helping to denote limits, helping to define and consolidate friendships, showing off sharpness in social discourse, and jostling for status. Pupils showed that considerable skill could be required in determining what form of teasing was appropriate with particular people.
>
> (Blatchford 1999: 111)

Through unsupervised play children are given the opportunity to acquire skills such as co-operation and competition that are mainly learned through interactions with equals. Unless children are given the opportunity to engage with each other without adults hovering over them they won't really learn the consequences of being clumsy, nasty or thoughtless, or how to cope with good-natured teasing or spiteful and hurtful behaviour.

Children are, of course, much less sophisticated than adults. But it is precisely for that reason that they need to be given the opportunity to create and resolve conflicts. Playing, fighting and stumbling into difficult situations – the very things adults rush to stop – help shape children into competent and independent-minded individuals.

At times, in play, children test society's codes – they may push the boundaries of what is seen as acceptable behaviour. It is understandable that adults want to intervene when they feel children are misbehaving, but it may not necessarily be the best thing to do. Of course adults need to set some boundaries. When a child is clearly being scared witless by other children, adult intervention is necessary. But the boundaries need to be very carefully drawn and applied if the benefits of play are not to be undermined.

Unsupervised play isn't just some kind of childhood luxury that kids can do without. It is vital for children's healthy emotional and social development. We do children no favours by protecting them from all those experiences that may be distressing, or even risky, and that come with everyday life. But we would do them a real favour by expecting more of them and gently easing them into living life to the full – even if it entails getting some emotional or physical bruises along the way.

SEVEN

VIRTUAL LIVES?

Media, brands and the MySpace generation

At roughly the mid-point of the twentieth century, the US media land-scape included TV, radio and records, movies, and print media. Fewer than five years into the twenty-first century, the media landscape encompasses broadcast, cable, and satellite TV, the TV remote control, the VCR, the DVR, print media (books, magazines, newspapers), various audio media (broadcast, satellite, and cable radio, tapes, CDs, digital recordings – all of which are now highly portable), personal computers and the various on-line activities they allow (e.g., World Wide Web, e-mail, instant messaging, gaming, music and video streaming), video games (both TV-based and handheld), and portable telephones that connect to the Internet and do most of what any digital screen will do.

(Kaiser Family Foundation report Generation M: Media in the Lives of 8–18 Year-olds*)*

There is a growing obsession on both sides of the Atlantic with what has been termed 'the commercialization of childhood'. Ed Balls, UK Secretary of State for Children, Schools and Families, announced in his 2007 Children's Plan: '[T]he Government will commission an independent assessment of the overall impact of the commercial world on children's well-being ... In particular, the assessment will

111

investigate particular areas where exposure to commercialism might be causing harm to children' (DCSF 2007a: 45).

The think-tank IPPR warned in its report *Freedom's Orphans*:

> Seven to eleven-year-olds are now worth nearly £20 million a year as consumers and have become an increasingly lucrative target audience for unscrupulous advertisers eager to harness their 'pester power' ... Research shows that rising affluence has had a pernicious effect on young people. As society has become richer, the impact on youth society has been to increasingly draw young people into consumerism.
>
> (IPPR 2006: ix)

The National Consumer Council (NCC) study titled *Shopping Generation* purportedly shows 'that many young people feel commercially abused and treated as second-class citizens by companies and advertisers' (Mayo 2005: 44). The NCC press release states:

> The new generation of young people aged ten to nineteen are avid shoppers, representing a £30 billion commercial market. They have more pocket money, more influence over family spending and more sway over social trends, but they believe they have little opportunity to shape the commercial world they live in.
>
> (NCC 8 July 2005)

The NCC survey found that the average ten-year-old has internalized between 300 and 400 brands.

According to Professor David Piachaud, at the Economic and Social Research Council (ESRC) Centre for Analysis of Social Exclusion at the London School of Economics, the commercialization of childhood has an immense impact on the psychological well-being of the nation's youth. 'One major factor in the commercialisation of childhood is that family earnings have nearly tripled in Britain over the past fifty years. The average disposable income per head of the population has risen from £3,789 in 1955 to £12,764 in 2005,' states the ESRC's corporate publication *The Edge* (Goodchild 2007: 14).

A big rise in disposable income sounds like pretty good news to me. But the problem is, apparently, that an increase in the purchasing power of the average family can be exploited through advertising – particularly with products aimed at children. As has been quoted extensively in the media, the average child in Britain now sees at least 10,000 adverts a year (BBC Online 9 December 2007). The figure regularly quoted for children in the US is 20,000 (Gantz *et al.* 2007). The Centre for Analysis of Social Exclusion (CASE) study claims that these adverts may be increasing family conflict because of 'the demands placed on adults to satisfy children's materialistic cravings' (Goodchild 2007: 14).

A 2008 public opinion poll published by the Children's Society, as part of its Good Childhood Inquiry, indicated unease among adults about the effect on children's well-being of an increasingly commercialized world (Children's Society 26 February 2008). The poll, conducted by GfK NOP, found that an 'overwhelming majority (90 per cent) of adults thought that advertising to children at Christmas puts pressure on parents to spend more than they can afford'. The Children's Society warned that 'This could put parents and families at risk of debt in the early months of the new year and beyond' (Children's Society 26 February 2008).

In the US a plethora of new books have recently been published with equally dire warnings about the dangers of commercialization. In *Consuming Kids: The Hostile Takeover of Childhood* Susan Linn, educational psychologist and co-founder of Campaign for Commercial-free Childhood, argues that children are now the focus of a 'marketing maelstrom' (Linn 2004). All aspects of their lives – their health, education, creativity, and values – are at risk of being compromised by their status in the market place, she argues. In 2006 Linn was awarded the prestigious 'Presidential Citation' by the American Psychological Association (APA) for her 'leadership in opposing marketing to children'. Presenting Linn with the award, APA president Gerald Koocher said, 'You have focused sharp attention on the rights of children to grow up, and the rights of parents to raise them, without undermining by rampant consumer manipulation.'

In *Born to Buy* US sociologist Juliet Schor argues that the 'average kindergartner' can identify 300 logos, and from as early as two years of age are 'bonded to brands' (Schor 2004). And in *The Hurried Child: Growing up Too Fast Too Soon* US child development expert David Elkind argues that 'advertisers hurry children into psychologically and nutritionally unhealthy consumerism', thereby undermining the very nature of childhood (Elkind 2007: 86).

But are children really slaves to advertising and branding? Ed Mayo, chief executive of the NCC, puts a more balanced perspective on this question in the NCC report *Shopping Generation*. He concedes that children's attachment to brands is not that new:

> Throughout the twentieth century, children were avid consumers of sweets, comics, movies and books. And any school playground today still operates as a showcase for the variety of entrepreneurial practices that children engage in – trading cards and toys, swapping food from lunchboxes, noting favours.
>
> (Mayo 2005: 5)

It is particularly the effect of advertising on children's food choices that has come under scrutiny in recent years. The Kaiser Family Foundation study *Food for Thought: Television Food Advertising to Children in the United States* found that food was the top product seen by children in adverts (Gantz *et al.* 2007). But how does food advertising affect children's eating habits?

Social psychologist Sonia Livingstone at the London School of Economics (LSE) carried out an extensive review of research available worldwide on advertising and children's food choices (Livingstone 2005). She writes that there is certainly 'ample evidence that hours spent watching television correlates with measures of poor diet, poor health and obesity, among both children and adults' (Livingstone 2005: 7). However, as she rightly argues, correlation does not equal causation, and one needs to carry out experiments – with proper controls – before making any judgements about whether advertising has had an effect on children's diet, body weight and health.

Having reviewed the research, including both correlational and experimental studies, Livingstone concludes that the 'measurable, direct effect of food promotion on children's food preferences, knowledge and behaviour is comparatively small' (Livingstone 2005: 15). In other words, advertising most likely does have *some* effect, but a comparatively small one, on children's choice of food. It is of course not surprising that adverts influence their target audience. The advertising industry would surely not spend millions of pounds advertising to children if there was no evidence that it had any effect whatsoever. But as Livingstone points out, it is possible that 'advertising and promotion serves more to reinforce or sustain existing levels of product awareness or interest than it does to increase them' (Livingstone 2005: 20).

Similarly David Buckingham, Director of the Centre for the Study of Children, Youth and Media at London's Institute of Education, who has been asked by the UK government to head the investigation into the commercialization of childhood, has written:

> As is often the case in such debates, commentators tend to blame the media ... But – as with violence – blaming the media always provides an easy option, and it gets attention for politicians who need to be seen to be 'doing something' about the problem.
>
> (Buckingham 2005: 3)

Buckingham challenges the increasingly common presentation of the child in policy discussions and the media as 'incompetent' and 'media-illiterate'. 'Research tends to show that children are well aware of the persuasive intentions of advertising from a relatively young age,' he argues (Buckingham 2005: 3). Conceding that there is some debate about the matter, he asserts: 'it is generally agreed that by the time they reach the age of eight, most children are capable of mobilising quite a cynical discourse about advertising' (Buckingham 2005: 3). Buckingham has interviewed children who will describe 'at length and in great detail, and with a good deal of hilarity' how adverts are 'full of lies', often selling 'rubbish', and how advertisers' claims are 'always exaggerated and false' (Buckingham 2005: 3).

Even if we accept that children are more cynical about adverts than is commonly believed, what about the claims that excessive consumerism is restricting their experiences and their imaginations?

David Elkind claims in *The Power of Play* that 'the sheer number of toys owned by contemporary children weakens the power of play-things to engage children in dramatic thinking. Abundance, like familiarity, breeds contempt' (Elkind 2007: 16). But there is no body of research to support this claim. It may be true that some children have more toys than they know what to do with. I have lost count of how many dolls my six-year-old niece has acquired. And no matter how expensive and amazing her last doll is, her appetite for further acquisitions seems insatiable. Yet she can recite the names of – and tell a story about – each and every one of the dolls. Her imagination and curiosity have not been stifled by her relative affluence, despite seeming to receive as many toys for one birthday as I had throughout my entire childhood. She can have hours of fun engrossed in her own little fantasy world, just as I could at her age.

At base, the current obsession with advertising and consumerism shows an unhealthy disdain for modern living and affluence, and a snobbish contempt for 'ignorant' 'materialistic' children, and 'weak' and 'inept' parents. Concerns about 'pester power', and families being torn apart by the demands placed on the parents to satisfy their children's 'materialistic cravings' assume that parents are incapable of saying 'no'.

Of course parents come under a lot of pressure from their children to buy the latest gadgets or the right brands of foodstuffs, drinks and clothes. But it is up to parents to decide the extent to which they give in to their children's requests and how much of a say they give them in what gets included in the supermarket trolley. I am often amazed at the amount of money my sisters spend on my nephews – in particular their clothes. But then again, although we often had to make do with hand-me-downs, our parents spent a lot more on us than their parents could ever afford to spend on them. Surely it is a good thing that society has become ever more affluent: that there is more disposable income today; and stuff like clothes and toys is a great deal cheaper?

Media saturation

In addition to 'rampant consumer manipulation', we are told that the media – the new media in particular – are also playing a sinister role in spreading everything from paedophilia and pornography to ADHD and bullying.

As Norman Lewis and Frank Furedi argue in the 2008 Futures Diagnosis report *Children's Real Digital World*:

> Throughout modern history, the introduction of new media has tended to provoke a sense of foreboding regarding new risks. Many of the fears – violence, stupefaction, vulgarisation – associated with what we now call the old media have been transposed to the new. However, the sheer variety of additional risks associated with the new media – bullying, harassment, paedophiles, pornography, cyber violence, addiction, loneliness, identity theft, stalking, giving out of family information to commercial interests – goes way beyond the relatively narrow range of problems linked to the old media.
>
> (Furedi and Lewis in press)

For instance, US educationalist Chris Mercogliano warns that 'electronic media have the power to hypnotize children and take possession of the psyches. [They] are so enticing and provide so much instant and effortless gratification that they are severely eroding kids' desire and ability to engage in real play (Mercogliano 2007: 113 and 121). Even more alarmingly, he continues:

> [N]ot only is the tidal wave of high-tech games and entertainment negatively influencing the quality of children's thinking and feeling

(to an extent yet to be fully measured and perhaps impossible to measure), but it is also potentially impairing their ability to have any thoughts at all.

(Mercogliano 2007:140)

Libby Purves, columnist for the *Times* (London), is no less trenchant in her criticisms of the impact of television:

Overmuch television has been linked by reputable researchers not only to unfitness but to short sight, poor attention span, premature sexualisation, violence, copycat bullying, celebrity worship, unreal expectations and inability to communicate. And that's before you even get to the ad break.

(Purves 11 December 2007)

How much truth is there in this growing denunciation of young people's media use? The media clearly play a more central part in young people's lives than ever before: to the point where, as a report by the Kaiser Family Foundation described, young people's homes – even their bedrooms – as 'saturated with media' (Roberts *et al.* 2005). What does this mean for children and young people? Are electronic media 'hypnotizing' them and eroding their ability to engage in 'real play', adversely affecting their health and well-being?

Pre-schoolers

In fact, hard evidence of the media's ominous effects on young children is sorely lacking. If we look at young children first, a study by the University of Sheffield implied that children under six years of age generally lead well balanced lives, 'with popular culture, media and new technologies playing an important, but not overwhelming role, in their leisure activities' (Marsh 2005: 5). The study showed that 29 per cent of the children had a television in their bedroom and 6 per cent had a computer in their room. On a typical day, the average amount of time they engaged in screen-based technologies (including watching television, videos or DVDs, using computers, playing console games and playing hand-held games, such as Gameboys) was two hours and six minutes. They spent an equal amount of time on a typical day playing with their toys. The researchers concluded:

> Often anxieties about media and young children are based on misinformation and nervousness about the prospect of a seemingly 'runaway world' in which children and young people are the 'digital insiders' and adults the outsiders, unsure about where the technology is leading and concerned about losing control.
>
> (Marsh 2005: 11)

US research and surveys indicate similar levels of media exposure for American children under six years of age. A study by the Kaiser Family Foundation entitled *Zero to Six: Electronic Media in the Lives of Infants, Toddlers and Pre-schoolers* found that 36 per cent of US children under six years of age – a slightly higher proportion than in the UK – had a television in their bedrooms (Rideout *et al.* 2003). Nearly three-quarters (73 per cent) had a computer at home, and about half (49 per cent) had a video game player. According to their parents, US pre-schoolers spent on average just under two hours a day with screen media, slightly less than UK children, and just over two hours a day playing outside.

The researchers also looked into whether watching television could legitimately be said to 'displace' other activities: that is, whether 'the time children spend watching TV replaces time they might spend in other pursuits, such as reading or playing outside' (Rideout *et al.* 2003: 9). They found that among the younger children – those from six months to three years of age – no such effect was found. However, among the older children – those between four and six years of age – 'the heavy TV watchers spent an average of thirty minutes less per day playing outside and eight minutes less per day reading than did children who were not heavy TV watchers' (Rideout *et al.* 2003: 9). But, as the researchers admit, 'it is not possible to tell from this study whether it is a causal relationship' (Rideout *et al.* 2003: 9). In other words, we cannot conclude that more television viewing *caused* the children to play outside less, or read less. One could equally infer that giving young children fewer opportunities to play outside was the reason they watched more television. Or, alternatively, that increased tele-viewing and decreased outdoor play may both have been due to some other unknown factor.

A study by Sonia Livingstone and Moira Bovill at the London School of Economics found: '[V]ery few children who viewed large amounts of television to the exclusion of other activities ... Nor did we find children so addicted to computer games that they had become socially isolated' (Livingstone and Bovill 1999: 19).

The claim that screen-based technologies are 'hypnotizing' or 'so enticing ... that they are severely eroding kids' desire and ability to engage in real play' is not held up by evidence – not for pre-school children, anyway.

What about possible effects on children's physical health? In August 1999, the American Academy of Pediatrics (AAP) issued guidelines urging parents to avoid television for children under two years of age:

> While certain television programs may be promoted to this age group, research on early brain development shows that babies and toddlers have a critical need for direct interactions with parents and other significant care givers for healthy brain growth and the development of appropriate social, emotional, and cognitive skills.

A later AAP study, appearing in the journal *Pediatrics*, allegedly showed that watching television as a toddler can lead to Attention Deficit Hyperactivity Disorder (ADHD) in later life (Christakis *et al.* 2004). Lead researcher, Dr Dimitri Christakis said, 'In contrast to the way real life unfolds and is experienced by young children, the pace of TV is greatly sped up' (Christakis *et al.* 2004: 709). He claimed that exposing a baby's developing brain to videos may overstimulate it, causing permanent changes in developing neural pathways; and that the damage shows up at seven years of age when children have difficulty paying attention in school.

The study of more than 2,000 children was widely interpreted as showing that, for every hour of television watched at one and three years of age, the children had almost a 10 per cent higher chance of developing ADHD by the age of seven. This 'evidence' has been reported uncritically by a growing army of researchers, commentators, writers and policymakers devoted to 'detoxing childhood'. But the study did not show that too much television at an early age increases the chance of developing ADHD. For a start, the children weren't formally diagnosed with ADHD. Instead, their parents were simply asked whether their child had difficulty concentrating, was easily confused, was impulsive, had trouble with obsessions or was restless. And, most important, just because the children who were judged by their parents and teachers as having problems concentrating also watched more television, it doesn't mean that television viewing was the reason they had problems paying attention. It could instead be that they already had ADHD, or just had difficulty concentrating, and got easily distracted by other activities, and therefore ended up watching more television. Subsequent research has not found a link between television viewing at a young age and ADHD.

The alleged links between television viewing, video and computer game use and unfitness and body fatness are equally tenuous. A meta-analysis – that is, a statistical technique for reviewing a large number of existing research studies – published in the *International Journal of Obesity* did find a statistically significant relationship between television viewing and body fatness for children between three and eighteen years of age, but one that was 'too small to be of substantial clinical relevance' (Marshall *et al.* 2004). The relationship between television viewing and physical activity was negative – that is, a higher amount of television viewing was linked with a lower amount of physical activity – but again the correlation was small. The researchers concluded that the studies to date did not demonstrate that excessive television viewing *caused* an increase in obesity or a decrease in physical activity.

The Myspace generation

What about older children? Are they so saturated in old and new media that their health, education, creativity and values are at risk of being compromised, as Mercogliano claims?

An LSE project by Sonia Livingstone and Magdalena Bober, summarized in the report *UK Children go Online*, found that most young people are daily or weekly users of the internet: 41 per cent are daily users and 43 per cent are weekly users. Most stay on line for less than an hour: 19 per cent spend about ten minutes per day on line and 48 per cent between half an hour and an hour (Livingstone and Bober 2005).

Two years later, the 2007 Monitor report, one of a series of annual surveys about children's media use produced by ChildWise, found a higher rate of internet use, this time among five to sixteen-year-olds. Users were found to spend an average of 1.9 hours a day on line (ChildWise 2007). This was coupled with a 'gradual downward trend in children's TV viewing ... with children watching an average of 2.4 hours per day, compared to three hours five years ago' (ChildWise 2007: 1). That means children and young people in the UK spend on average just over four hours a day in front of computer and television screens. And in 2008 OfCom, the regulator and competition authority for the UK communications industries, found that almost half (49 per cent) of children aged eight to seventeen who use the internet had set up their own profile on a social networking site. Despite the minimum age for most major social networking sites being thirteen or above, over a quarter (27 per cent) of eight to eleven-year-olds who were aware of social networking sites said that they had set up a profile.

The US report *Generation M: Media in the Lives of 8–18 Year-olds* found that children and young people's average television exposure exceeded three hours a day (Roberts *et al.* 2005). When all screen media (including DVDs and movies) were included the average daily exposure climbed to four and a half hours. The amount of time the eight to eighteen-year-olds used computers for 'recreational purposes' (that is, not including school use) was just over an hour per day (an hour and two minutes). On the other hand, fewer than half spent thirty minutes or more with print media, and on any given day only one-fifth devoted more than an hour to reading for leisure. Television exposure decreased with age, while computer use increased with age.

The amount of time young people spend in front of television and computer screens clearly amounts to quite a large chunk of their day. But if children are spending too many hours on 'sedentary screen play' we should ask ourselves why that is. Ed Mayo, chief executive of the National Consumer Council, wrote in an online debate on *spiked* about social networking: 'The consumer freedoms of mobile telephony and social networking are valued precisely because these are innovations which promise autonomy and a release from adult control' (Mayo 2006).

If children are not allowed to mess around with their friends out-doors, away from adult supervision, they will look for other means of circumventing adult control. This is a worldwide phenomenon. Technology analyst Norman Lewis argues on *spiked*:

> Like their counterparts in the West, young people in Asia are adopting [new] technologies into their lives because of their lived experience of childhood … In both parts of the world, children's lives are increasingly controlled and under the gaze of adults. While risk consciousness in the West has resulted in what some have characterised as the rise of bedroom culture and its accompanying decline of street culture, in Asia young people's lives are equally structured and controlled. The attraction of digital media in both parts of the world is frequently shaped by children's desire to create their own space and enjoy a measure of independence from adult control.
>
> (Lewis 19 May 2008)

Teens are looking for ways of socializing with their peers while being confined – much more than our generation was – to their homes. Indeed, *UK Children go Online* shows that young people's main motivation for going on line is to hang out with their friends (Livingstone and Bober 2005). Most online communication is with people they have face-to-face contact with on a regular basis: 'Being in constant contact with friends is highly valued, and there is little interest contacting strangers,' the report states (Livingstone and Bober 2005: 4).

A 2006 national survey of teenagers conducted by the Pew Internet and American Life Project found that more than half (55 per cent) of US youngsters between twelve and seventeen years of age use social networking sites such as MySpace and Facebook (Lenhart *et al.* 2007). As with the UK youth surveyed for *UK Children go Online*, most of them (91 per cent) said they use the sites to stay in touch with friends they see frequently. As Danah Boyd, popular blogger and internet researcher with the School of Information (iSchool) at the University of California, writes, 'When I ask teenagers why they joined MySpace, the answer is simple: "Cuz that's where my friends are." Their explanation of what they do on the site is much more vague: "I don't know ... I just hang out"' (Boyd 2007: 9).

Boyd writes:

> What teens are doing with this networked public is akin to what they have done in every other type of public they have access to: they hang out, jockey for social status, work through how to present themselves, and take risks that will help them to assess the boundaries of the social world.
>
> (Boyd 2007: 21)

Her research led her to the conclusion that, in essence, MySpace is the 'civil society' of teenage culture: 'whether one is for it or against it, everyone knows the site and has an opinion about it' (Boyd 2007: 3).

Do the new media put children at greater risk from paedophilia, pornography and bullying? In the UK consultation document *Staying Safe*, Ed Balls, Secretary of State for Children, Schools and Families, conceded, 'Growth in new technologies has brought wonderful new opportunities for education, information, communication and leisure.' 'But,' warned Balls, 'it also brings new opportunities for people who wish to harm children – for example through online grooming, sharing abusive images or as a means to bully other children and young people' (DCSF 2007b: 3).

However, in the government-commissioned report entitled *Safer Children in a Digital World* clinical psychologist and television super-nanny Tanya Byron admits that the 'concrete "evidence" of harm resulting from the internet is fairly limited' (Byron 2008: 59). Similarly, research carried out by OfCom showed that:

> The majority of comments in our qualitative sample were positive about social networking. A few users did mention negative aspects to social networking, and these included annoyance at others using sites for self-promotion, parties organised on line getting out of hand, and online bullying.
>
> (OfCom 2008: 10)

A literature review compiled for OfCom shows that 'there is a lack of information about any actual harm (as opposed to risk of harm) experienced by users of social networking sites' (OfCom 2008: 12).

Of course, where there is freedom – as with the relatively unregulated worldwide web – there will always be 'opportunities' for abusers and criminals. But, interestingly, research indicates that children and young people may be a little bit more savvy than most policy-makers and the child protection industry assume. *UK Children go Online* found that almost one-third (30 per cent) of the youngsters had made 'an online acquaintance', and 8 per cent said they had 'met face to face with someone whom they first met on the internet' (Livingstone and Bober 2005). But the vast majority (89 per cent) told someone they were going to the meeting beforehand and 67 per cent took a friend with them. Six per cent said that the person they met turned out to be different from what they expected, but the vast majority had a good time, with 91 per cent saying that the meeting was 'good' or 'okay'.

Children and young people will inevitably need to learn how to negotiate certain risks on line. There is always the possibility that some sinister person will attempt to 'groom' a child or young person.

But every arena of our lives poses potential risks, which ultimately we all need to learn to negotiate rather than try to eliminate. As Danah Boyd said at symposium organized by the American Association for the Advancement of Science, 'There *are* potential risks on MySpace but it is important not to exaggerate them. The risks are not why youth are flocking to the site. To them, the benefits for socialisation outweigh the potential harm' (Boyd 2006). Boyd argued that, although letting go and allowing youth to navigate risks is terrifying for parents, 'it's necessary for youth to mature'.

Most research indicates that children are quite savvy and able to identify those adults who try to pass themselves off as children. It would be a real shame if the frantic desire to protect children from the shadowy figures who might wish to harm them threatened one of the few arenas young people have left to conduct relationships with each other outside the increasingly closely monitored worlds of home and school.

PART III

TAKING REAL RESPONSIBILITY

The role of adult society

EIGHT

LET PARENTS BE PARENTS
The myth of infant determinism

Children begin by loving their parents; as they grow older they judge them; sometimes, they forgive them.

(Oscar Wilde, 1891)

Parents are continually told how difficult parenting is – 'the toughest thing anyone faces in their personal life', writes former UK Prime Minister Tony Blair in the *Sun* newspaper (Blair 21 November 2006) – and how likely they are to mess up if they don't seek expert advice. During a stay at a Thai boxing camp in Thailand a fellow boxer told me he was put into care as a toddler. He wondered whether his mother's alcoholism was likely to have damaged him, 'because they say the first three years make you who you are, don't they?'

Well, they do say that – but that doesn't make it true.

Infant determinism – the idea that who we are is determined by experiences in the first years of our lives – is all-pervasive. Back in 1997 Hillary Clinton, then First Lady of the United States, drew on developments in neuroscience to set the tone for the popular debate. At a White House conference she asserted that experiences in infancy are responsible for the development of 'capacities that will shape the entire rest of their lives', and will 'determine how their brains are wired'. Experiences in the first three years, said Clinton, 'can determine whether children will grow up to be peaceful or violent citizens, focused or undisciplined workers, attentive or detached parents themselves' (Clinton 4 February 1997).

In 2004 the psychotherapist Sue Gerhardt argued in her much feted book *Why Love Matters: How Affection Shapes a Baby's Brain* that there is no such thing as a 'difficult baby', there are only 'difficult parents', who are either 'neglectful' or 'intrusive'. She warned that a lack of parental sensitivity in infancy will create problems when the child grows up – limiting the ability to respond to stress in adulthood, and increasing susceptibility to conditions such as depression, addiction and anorexia (Gerhardt 2004). Gerhardt writes: 'There is something powerful about the earliest themes of our lives, which chaos theory may help to explain. It suggests that small differences at the beginning of a process can lead to hugely different outcomes' (Gerhardt 2004: 15).

And if, as we are constantly reminded, the world is full of neglectful parents, the consequences are potentially disastrous. 'Health workers on home visits frequently report seeing mothers with a baby in one hand and a mobile phone in another, or failing to make eye contact with their suckling infant because they're simultaneously checking their e-mail or watching *Oprah* on TV,' Sue Palmer writes in *Toxic Childhood* (Palmer 2006: 111).

Oliver James, clinical psychologist and media pundit similarly argues in *They F*** You Up: How to Survive Family Life* that people are the victims of their childhood experiences (James 2002). Drawing on Philip Larkin's famous poem 'This be the verse' ('They fuck you up, your mum and dad. / They may not mean to, but they do. / They fill you with the faults they had / And add some extra, just for you') James argues that everything from addiction, personality disorder, violence and criminality, neurosis and hyperactivity can be traced back to the type of care received by a child between the ages of six months and three years.

James's book provoked something of a backlash, maybe because he went a bit too far in attacking parents for most people's liking. When the book was published, in September 2002, James ended up in a bitter row with Steven Pinker, US neuroscientist and popular science writer. James accused Pinker, author of *The Blank Slate*, of promoting a 'wicked' argument by downplaying the impact of our upbringing on our lives, giving the 'perfect excuse to be violent to children' (as if there are all these people who are just waiting for the right excuse to beat their children). Judith Rich Harris, author of *The Nurture Assumption*, jumped to Pinker's defence – pronouncing that James's parents must have done a bad job in bringing him up, and that 'certainly, he sounds fucked-up, like his book'. This must have been particularly wounding for James, who prides himself on the fact that his parents went through years of psychoanalytic treatment to ensure they were good enough to raise their kids.

The crux of James's argument is that our emotional attachments in the first years of our lives shape all our future relationships, as well as our sense of self. The only way any of us can survive a less than perfect upbringing, he argues, is through years of psychotherapy or drug treatment. Not everybody agreed with that argument, either. In a *British Medical Journal* review of James's previous book, *Britain on the Couch: Why we're Unhappier Compared with 1950 despite being Richer*, Simon Wessely, Professor of Epidemiological and Liaison Psychiatry at King's College School of Medicine in London, threw cold water on the wonders of drug therapy: 'Despite James's enthusiasm, his knowledge of psychopharmacology is somewhat superficial ... [B]elieving that serum serotonin levels tell us anything about central serotonin is like watching the sky in London to guess the weather in Sydney' (Wessely 1998: 83).

James also argues governments have a key role to play in improving family life. For a start, he argues, policymakers should replace the obsession with economic performance indicators with greater measurement of the effect of government policy on mental health: 'Every two years there should be a nationally representative audit ... by which the government should be judged. This audit would include an evaluation of how parenting is faring in the light of government policy' (James, 2002: 300).

For New Labour to set such targets would be entirely in character – and there is certainly no shortage of government initiatives to try to improve the nation's parenting skills. One can only wonder whether a parent getting lower-than-estimated grades would have recourse to a re-mark. Although, how one could measure the 'success' in improving such an intimate aspect of life as family relationships is anybody's guess.

Much of James's book is rehashed pop psychology: conjecture presented as authoritative fact. Take his claim that 'offspring of families with five or more children are significantly more likely to be delinquent and to suffer mental illness' (James 2002: 4). Why? Because there is not enough love to go round. That's me (and my four siblings) screwed, for a start. Or take his claim that:

> [A]t least as big a determinant as gender of the role in which your parents cast you in the family drama is your place in the family, known as birth order ... [F]irstborn children are more likely to be self-assured, assertive, competitive and dominant compared with lastborns.
>
> (James 2002: 41)

'Lastborns,' says James, 'are more altruistic, emotionally empathetic and, when small, get more involved with other children' (James 2002: 41). Of course James can present numerous examples to support this thesis – and each and every one of us could find numerous examples to challenge it.

One cannot help but feel that James gives the family, and parents in particular, an unfairly hard time. It's ironic that he pleads with the reader:

> [P]lease believe me when I say that the last thing I want to do through this book is stir up trouble between you and your family, to burst the bubble of illusions you have about your own childhood or to add to the burden of anxiety that parents already carry.
>
> (James 2002: 10)

How else are parents supposed to react to a book that preaches the ease with which they could destroy their children's lives – just by falling short of a smile or two?

Attachment theory

Infant determinists, such as Sue Gerhardt and Oliver James, invariably draw on work by the late UK psychiatrist John Bowlby at the Tavistock Clinic in London in the 1950s and 1960s. He argued that an important difference between 'vulnerable' and 'resilient' children is found in the quality of their earliest relationships, particularly attachment to a mother figure (Bowlby 1969). A secure relationship with their care-giver makes children more secure and able to cope with stressful situations later in life, claimed Bowlby; while children who haven't developed secure attachments in infancy fail to develop lasting relationships as adults.

The reality is that it is far from obvious how early attachments shape our development. It is extremely difficult to isolate variables in longitudinal studies of human behaviour, which follow participants over an extended period of time. Quantifying the effect of childhood experiences on adult life is almost impossible. It is undoubtedly the case that we are influenced by the care we receive in infancy. Childhood experiences do play their part in informing our attitudes and behaviour in later life, and our personalities start taking shape at an early age.

And of course our family relationships are likely to play a big role in shaping ourselves. Our relationships with our parents and siblings are, after all, the longest, most enduring relationships many of us will have – they tend to be for life. But they do not determine who we are: just as we may form relationships outside the home that affirm our sense of self and nature of attachment, so we may form relationships that challenge our self-image and our way of relating to other people. We may be *shaped* by childhood experiences but we are not *determined* by them in the sense of early experiences irreversibly shaping the rest of our lives.

The bulk of empirical research on attachment security builds on the work of the psychologist Mary Ainsworth and her colleagues, who devised the experimental procedure known as 'Strange Situation' as a test of children's attachment security (Ainsworth *et al.* 1978). In the Strange Situation test, children are subjected to a number of mild stresses – such as being left alone with a stranger – in order to assess their feelings towards their care-giver. Ainsworth claimed that the data showed children could be categorized into three basic attachment types: secure; insecure/avoidant or 'indifferent'; and insecure/resistant or 'clingers'. The differences between the attachment types was seen to be influenced by the care-giver's sensitivity during interactions in early infancy. Also, the attachment types were seen as relatively stable, and to have some predictive power with regard to children's future emotional development.

When we look at the empirical research, though, it is far from clear-cut. Some studies have indeed demonstrated that attachment classifications in very young children – between twelve and eighteen months of age – are relatively stable (Waters 1978). Other studies have found that just over 50 per cent of children obtained the same attachment classification before their second birthday as they obtained at twelve months (Thompson *et al.* 1982). Also, the link between the attachment types and later outcomes is very unclear. As Rudolph Schaffer, Professor of Psychology at the University of Strathclyde, said, 'Prediction over a period of several years is always hazardous, and especially so because of the uncontrolled influences of intervening events' (Schaffer 1996: 147).

Having carried out an extensive review of the attachment literature, Schaffer concludes: 'Children no doubt differ in the quality of the attachment relationships they form; however, the issue of the ante-cedents of such differences and their consequences is nowhere near as straightforward as has been suggested by many attachment enthusiasts' (Schaffer 1996: 148).

So the research has not established a link between parenting styles and types of attachment, nor has it shown that there are 'critical periods' for emotional and social development.

The use and abuse of neuroscience

It is often argued that recent research in neuroscience gives weight to the idea that we are determined by the attention we receive as babies.

The brain produces an immense number of synapses (neural connections) in the first few years of a child's life. After this there is a prolonged period of 'pruning', or withering away, of synapses. But neuroscience has not come up with any clear answers as to how synaptic circuits are shaped or altered by experience. There is no firm evidence demonstrating that the type of care received in infancy has an effect on synaptogenesis – the creation of new synapses – or on synaptic pruning. These processes take place regardless of infants' experiences.

In 1999 the US National Center for Early Development and Learning (NCEDL) convened a working conference, 'Critical Thinking about Critical Periods', bringing together recognized experts from the fields of neuroscience and early child development to evaluate the evidence for 'critical periods' of early life. In the book of the same title that came out of the conference Donald Bailey, Professor of Education at the University of North Carolina, notes that 'parents, educators, policy makers, and early childhood advocates share, with greater or lesser understanding, the concept of critical "windows of opportunity" early in development' (Bailey 2001: xiii). However, he also argues: '[W]e have too much evidence about the remarkable ability of humans to change and learn from experience at virtually every age to conclude that the early childhood years are necessarily more important than other years.'

If there are critical periods, they are 'critical' only in the sense that a complete absence of stimuli during this period could have irreversible negative consequences. As John Bruer, President of the James S. McDonnell Foundation and author of the 1999 book *The Myth of the First Three Years*, said on *Frontline*, the US flagship public affairs television series, '[W]hat we have to realize is the kind of experience we need during that critical period is everywhere around us. It is not something we have to go out and provide children.'

Similarly, neuroscientist Steve Petersen at Washington University argues that the environment would have to be very bad to interfere with a child's normal neurological development. His tongue-in-cheek advice to parents is 'Don't raise your child in a closet, starve them, or hit them on the head with a frying pan' (Bruer 1999: 188).

US psychologists David Anderegg persuasively shows that what we have learnt from brain research is this:

> Practically speaking, one could argue that the best recommendation to come out of the new brain research is that neglect is bad for children; it is not only bad for children's emotional life, but also bad, apparently, for their neurophysiological life. So the best, safest, most clear recommendation here would be: Don't neglect your children. Don't leave them in their cribs for hours at a time with nothing to look at. Do talk to them. Don't leave them alone for days on end. Do touch them, wash them, and play with them. Do something with them.
>
> (Anderegg 2004: 41)

Romanian orphanages

Proponents of 'critical periods' will often draw on examples from the Romanian orphanages to demonstrate the importance of early emotional engagements. After the fall of the Ceauşescu regime in 1989, many were stunned by the images that emerged from Romania's state orphanages. The children had suffered extreme deprivation: they were malnourished and many were crippled by being tied to their cots for months on end. They had been given no individual attention other than minimal routine physical care. They were passive and emotionless and, in most of the kids, developmental delay was obvious.

What is less often recalled is that, remarkably, studies of children reared in these orphanages and adopted by US, Canadian and British parents found a phenomenal degree of catch-up (Rutter 1998; Benoit et al. 1996). Also, contrary to attachment theorists' predictions, the children were able to form attachments to their adoptive parents. Rudolph Schaffer concluded, 'The pattern of [the] findings as a whole underlines the remarkable resilience of development that is possible after early and severe deprivation' (Schaffer 2004: 338).

Nonetheless, a higher than average proportion of the children were insecurely attached: being overly 'clingy' with their care-givers and often inappropriately friendly with strangers. And the children reared in the orphanages and adopted after their first birthday were less likely to fully recover psychologically than those adopted at a younger age.

It may well be the case that extreme emotional deprivation in the first two years of life can have devastating and irreversible consequences. But it is exceptionally rare to see children subjected to anything like the appalling treatment of those Romanian orphans. Extreme conditions of emotional deprivation may be so exceptional that they tell us absolutely nothing about the situations where there is engagement between adult and child. There is a world of difference between being starved of human contact and having parents who do not match up to attachment enthusiasts' expectations – being continually loving, caring, expressive, and encouraging. The mistake often made is to conflate occasionally clumsy or unresponsive parental behaviour with systematic abuse and neglect.

Every Child Matters: hard cases make bad law

In January 2001 at the Old Bailey in London Marie Therese Kouao and her boyfriend Carl Manning were sentenced to life imprisonment for the murder of eight-year-old Victoria Climbié. Victoria had frozen to death, and her skeletal body was covered in 128 horrific injuries. The child was seen by a number of social workers and police officers before she died, but they all failed to act to save Victoria's life.

Clearly, the social services and police failed to pick up on what was staring them in the face and were rightly condemned in court for being 'blindingly incompetent'. The subsequent inquiry into Victoria's death, chaired by Lord Laming, was damning not only of the four boroughs that dealt with the case, but also of the police child protection teams, the National Society for the Prevention of Cruelty to Children (NSPCC), and the doctors and nurses who were alerted to the potential abuse (Laming 2003). So how could this appalling catalogue of incompetence on the part of those purported to protect children at risk be allowed to happen?

It is not as if society worries too little about child abuse. Indeed, there is an army of child protection officers, care workers, high-profile children's charities and police units, aided by National Health Service workers and schoolteachers, all of whom are trained to spot 'hidden' signs of potential abuse in children, and to act upon it at the earliest possible opportunity. But, as Victoria's death indicated, this is part of the problem.

When those charged with protecting children are obsessed with finding hidden signs of abuse everywhere, there is a danger they will miss the blindingly obvious signs. But unfortunately this was not the lesson learnt from the inquiry. Instead a raft of recommendations – 108 in total – were put forward, involving a massive shake-up of the welfare services, including more appropriate training for social services staff.

But if child protection officers need training to recognize abuse in a malnourished child – covered in bruises, cigarette burns and open sores, including a belt-buckle mark indented on her body and hammer blows to her toes – then children at risk will never receive the protection they need. In fact, a number of adults *not* trained in child protection, who had come into contact with Victoria, including neighbours, had raised concerns about the child's welfare and the likelihood of abuse.

Mary Marsh, NSPCC Director, argued at the time that the brutal killing of Victoria – although one of the worst cases of abuse heard in a UK court – was not an isolated incident. One or two children die every week at the hands of their parents or carers, she pointed out. The deaths of one or two children at the hands of those who are supposed to be caring for them is one or two deaths too many. But it should be recognized that this figure amounts to fewer than one in 100,000 children over the course of a year. When investigating how to protect children against the risk of abuse, we also need to take account of the interests of the well over 99 per cent of children whose lives are not 'at risk'.

Furthermore, by failing to focus attention on those children who are at risk, there is a greater danger that those children fall through the net, such as seven-year-old Khyra Ishaq, who starved to death in her home in Birmingham, England, in May 2008. In this sense, drawing 'broader lessons' for society may do more harm than good for children like Victoria and Khyra. But that's precisely what the government did in the 2003 Green Paper *Every Child Matters*, which was motivated by the Laming inquiry. *Every Child Matters* represents, in the words of then Prime Minister, Tony Blair, 'the most far-reaching reform of child services for thirty years': a shift from targeted services that respond to particular crises to an emphasis on prevention, and maximizing opportunities for all children. The policy document's recommendations included integrating teams of health and education professionals and social workers based in and around schools and children's centres, and sweeping away legal technical and cultural barriers to information sharing, so that there could be effective communication between everyone with a responsibility for children.

The legal underpinning for *Every Child Matters* was provided by the Children Act 2004. This Act has given the government the power to create a database to store information on *all* children from birth, to be shared among all those agencies and officials involved in a child's life. But as a commissioner at the Information Commissioner's office has asked, 'When you're looking for a needle in a haystack, is it necessary to keep building bigger haystacks?'

Every Child Matters has shifted the focus from intervention in cases of grave hardship or vulnerability to an increasingly hands-on approach to family life in general. Speaking in March 2007, Alan Johnson, Secretary of State for Education and Skills, made this explicit: 'Traditionally, parenting has been a "no go" area for governments. But now more than ever government needs to be supportive of parents who are themselves increasingly seeking help' (Directgov 15 March 2007).

In December 2007 Ed Balls, Secretary of State for Children, Schools and Families, wrote in the ten-year *Children's Plan*, '[B]uilding on a decade of reform and results, and responding directly to [parent's] concerns, our Children's Plan will strengthen support for all families during the formative early years of their children's lives' (DCSF 2007a: 3).

We may wonder how the tragic death of one child, in a case of abuse so horrific that it shocked the nation, has led so rapidly and seamlessly to the notion that all parents and all children need monitoring, surveillance and government 'support' in their everyday family lives. As David Clements, who works in children's social care, has argued on *spiked*:

> [N]ever before has a government's response to a child's death been so sweeping in its implications for all children and families. The new agenda is about prevention, early intervention and safeguarding – in other words, protecting children from innumerable risks to their well-being, not just (or even predominantly) abuse or neglect.
>
> (Clements 4 October 2007)

This will not do much to help children 'at risk' and those currently in care. Clements, quite rightly, argues, 'There are exceptions when society, one way or another, must intervene to protect or care for a child. But these instances are rare and must be treated as such.'

When such exceptional cases as that of Victoria Climbié are used to argue for placing the overwhelming majority of non-abusive families under suspicion, this can only undermine the spontaneous relationships and the human contact that could well have saved Victoria's life. It was not the absence of legal regulations that caused Victoria to die, as the trial judge put it, 'a lonely drawn-out death'. It was the lack of two very human characteristics: compassion and common sense. And these two qualities – compassion and common sense – are continually being eroded by government policies and the burgeoning parenting industry, which has been given a new lease of life with *Every Child Matters*.

The parenting industry

In 2004 psychotherapist Sue Gerhardt argued that government initiatives should be targeted 'at the point where it can make the most difference' – 'during pregnancy and in the first two years of life' (Gerhardt 2004: 3). She was pushing at an open door. In November 2006 the Prime Minister, Tony Blair, pledged to spend £4 million of his Respect Task Force budget on sending a team of 'parenting experts' into Britain's most deprived areas. The seventy or so 'super-nannies' were to help struggling parents control their antisocial children, Blair claimed in an article in the *Sun* newspaper (Blair 21 November 2006). The government is also funding the creation of the National Academy for Parenting Practitioners, with the express aim of training a 'parenting work force' to provide reliable child-rearing advice to the mums and dads of the nation.

In November 2006 Beverley Hughes, UK Minister for Children, Young People and Families, argued at a National Family and Parenting Institute (NFPI) conference at which I was presenting a paper that parents have lost confidence in their ability to bring up their children properly. The government must take a lead, she argued, and offer parents 'empowering, practical support' to 'unlock children's full potential'. One way the government will do this, said Hughes, is by providing parents with lessons in how to sing nursery rhymes – in order to help to get children off to 'a flying start' (Hughes 13 November 2006).

Not surprisingly, Hughes's nursery rhyme intervention was derided by commentators as intrusive and patronizing. 'Think Mao's cultural revolution, but led by Wee Willie Winkie,' wrote one *Daily Telegraph* columnist scathingly. But Hughes is not alone in thinking parents need training in how to play with their children. Stevanne Auerbach, affectionately known in the US as 'Dr Toy', and author of the 1998 book *Smart Play, Smart Toys: How to Raise a Child with a High PQ – Play Quotient*, says her goal is to 'encourage parents to understand that they are their children's first big toy' (Shea 15 July 2007).

The parenting industry clearly thinks that it knows what is best for other people's children. But, as I have argued, much of what goes for 'expert advice' today is based on flawed assumptions. And we should remember that, as anthropologist David Lancy argued in the journal *American Anthropologist*, parent–child play is only really found among the upper and middle classes in wealthy countries (Lancy 2007). In most cultures adults think it is rather silly to play with children, he states. I am sure he is right. I have hours of fun playing with my niece and nephews, and engage in what – in some cultures – must seem like very strange behaviour. In many ways it is, but there is no harm in playing with children. Neither should adult–child play be presented as an essential ingredient in children's development. When it comes to children's play, the most important thing is to give them the opportunity to develop their own fantasy worlds and make up their own games with their own rules.

Yet in the US many cities and states support programmes that aim to 'spread adult–child play beyond its traditional stronghold'. The *Boston Globe* reported in July 2007 that staff from the Parent–Child Home Program will visit the homes of low-income residents in Massachusetts 'and offer tips not just on good books for toddlers but also on "play activities" for parents and kids' (Shea 15 July 2007).

Undermining parents' confidence

When parents need advice on how to play with their children, is it any wonder that they, as Beverley Hughes pointed out, seem to be losing confidence in their abilities? A survey in 2004, funded by the Scottish Executive, found that a high proportion of parents lack confidence in their ability as parents. This MORI poll, which asked more than 1,000 adults about their views on parenting, found that almost a quarter of parents 'worry all the time' about whether or not they are doing a good job. A further 16 per cent are concerned 'quite a lot of the time' (Meiklem 24 October 2004).

But Hughes should ask herself why this might be the case. Could it be that endless government initiatives intervening in the minutiae of family life have contributed to a continuing erosion of parents' self-confidence? It makes you wonder how parents have managed through the ages before New Labour came into existence. The fact is, as well as throwing up all kinds of new challenges, parenting can be immensely enjoyable and fulfilling. Surely all the government pronouncements about the potential pitfalls of parenting only serve to undermine the joys of family life?

That is not to say that parents cannot benefit from helpful tips on common challenges – such as how to deal with toddlers throwing tantrums in the local supermarket, or how to deal with a child who refuses to go to bed. But the widespread idea that parents must always seek expert advice or risk raising 'damaged' children who will then do damage to society – an idea continually promoted by government officials, television gurus and numerous newspaper and magazine articles – only contributes to feelings of uncertainty among parents.

In *The Story of Childhood* Libby Brooks recounts her conversations with nine very different children between the ages of four and sixteen growing up in 'today's ASBO-afflicted Britain' (Brooks 2006). One of the children is teenage mum Lauren – 'a child who is also a parent, a totem for liberal despair and conservative vitriol' (Brooks 2006: 305). Lauren seems quite a determined and bright girl: she is busy studying for her ten GCSEs, despite the school telling her she could drop some. And she is not impressed with parenting classes, saying:

> It's just trial and error. You go to parenting class and they're telling you what they think is the right way. But there's no right or wrong way of doing it. At least if you do things wrong it makes things better because you learn from your mistakes.
>
> (Brooks 2006: 330)

She tries to do her best and is confident that is good enough. No doubt she is right.

In July 2007 Mary Morgan, widow of child care guru Dr Benjamin Spock, famous for his best-selling tome *Baby and Child Care*, published in 1945, told *spiked* that her late husband would be horrified by the avalanche of advice that parents are buried under today:

> What we've done with experts in parenting is to tell people that they don't know anything, and they have to rely on somebody that's done this and done that. We undermine some of the

greatest wisdom we've had handed to us: what we know intuitively. I'm not saying that the experts are wrong. I just think that this attitude has weakened the self-confidence of parents.

(McDermott July 2007)

The opening phrase of *Baby and Child Care*, in stark contrast to today's parenting advice, is 'Trust yourself. You know more than you think you do.' Morgan argues that the book was more of a reassurance for parents, as opposed to the new-style parenting books from the 1980s onwards that 'shake their fingers and say, "Listen, if you don't do exactly what I say, you're going to kill your kid"' (McDermott July 2007). Spock worried about his effect on parents, recalls Morgan: '[He] said this many times that there's less confidence among parents now than there ever has been ... He blamed all the experts that told parents they're doing it wrong' (McDermott July 2007).

As the US psychologist David Anderegg perceptively points out in his book *Worried all the Time: Discovering the Joy in Parenting in an Age of Anxiety*, 'Overparenting is trying to make perfect decisions every single time, in a world that is much more indeterminate and forgiving than most parents believe' (Anderegg 2003: 4). He adds, 'Parenting is one of those things that really works when you stop trying so hard; most often, you can really be a good parent when you let go of the effort and stop worrying about the outcome' (Anderegg 2003: 211).

Similarly Christina Hardyment, author of *Dream Babies: Childcare Advice from John Locke to Gina Ford*, has warned that parents are feeling 'hypnotized and disempowered by both the abundance and contradictions of all the advice, especially when claims are made ... that certain practices can permanently damage, even threaten, the lives of babies' (Hardyment 24 December 2007). Her advice is to survey the parenting books with the same subjectivity we use when we select a magazine or a cookery book. 'Opt for an approach that suits you,' she advises. '[T]he odds are that your baby – because it is yours – will like it too' (Hardyment 24 December 2007).

The cradle of thought

In his perceptive book *The Cradle of Thought: Exploring the Origins of Thinking*, psychotherapist Peter Hobson reviews an array of clinical and experimental studies looking at the role of early emotional engagements in our development (Hobson 2004). He argues that it is out of the cradle of these early emotional engagements that the ability to have thoughts emerges. Once emotional engagements have developed into symbolic communication, the child leaves infancy behind, Hobson argues, and, 'empowered by language and other forms of symbolic functioning, [the child] takes off into the realms of culture. The infant has been lifted out of the cradle of thought. Engagement with others has taught this soul to fly' (Hobson 2004: 274).

Hobson presents a far more intelligent and interesting account of the role of early relationships than any infant determinist. Engagement between the adult and the child should be seen as a stepping-stone, he writes, to the future transformation of the child. Where the engagement is completely absent, the consequences can be devastating. But the vast majority of adults will be emotionally sensitive and responsive to their children.

Extrapolating from cases of extreme neglect only serves to guilt-trip parents into believing that if they should mess up – even temporarily – there will be no second chance, and their children will be on the fast track to failure.

Of course, some parents will be awkward in the way they show their love for their children; others will fail to provide enough praise and encouragement. But even if emotional sensitivity is lacking, Hobson argues, 'one is constantly amazed by the resilience of babies and how effectively they can find ways round potential disadvantage and get much of what they need from people around them' (Hobson 2004: 149). Much research contradicts the pessimistic belief in irreversible influences in early childhood, showing instead that children are pretty resilient psychologically.

The reality is that we cannot predict with any certainty how someone is going to turn out on the basis of what kind of childhood they had. That's the beauty of being human – we are all unique. We are adaptable, yet unpredictable. It is, of course, possible to gain insights into how some things are likely to influence our lives, but we are not able to chart out with any degree of certainty exactly how any of us will turn out as adults.

Infant determinists have had a significant impact in policy circles on both sides of the Atlantic, not because of the strength of their arguments but because their perspective fits in with today's cultural outlook that views adults as 'emotionally illiterate' and in constant need of a helping hand. Parenting is too important to be left in the realm of the private and personal, we are told. But undermining parents' common sense, which has been quite good enough for generations, is more likely to damage parent–child relationships than occasional instances of Mum and Dad doing or saying the 'wrong' thing. The more parents are led to believe that they are likely to mess up unless they seek expert advice the more stilted and insecure they are likely to become in the way they relate to their children.

Parent–child relationships are shaped and sustained through a unique and enduring love – a love that, in the vast majority of cases, is healthily expressed through spontaneous emotional interactions. If parents are led to believe that they need to follow a set script in order to engage with children in a non-destructive way, then ultimately they will be held back from expressing loving, compassionate and empathic feelings.

Those genuinely concerned about the future well-being of today's generation of children should stop castigating parents for everything they do. It would be more constructive to counter all the various initiatives – often led by governments and state authorities – which undermine our trust in other adults and children. Free from such scaremongering and hectoring from the authorities, parents might learn to trust themselves and each other more.

NINE

LET TEACHERS BE TEACHERS – NOT SOCIAL WORKERS AND 'HAPPINESS COUNSELLORS'

It is, in fact, nothing short of a miracle that the modern methods of instruction have not entirely strangled the holy curiosity of inquiry.

(*Albert Einstein*)

When I worked as a primary school teacher in Gorton, Manchester, in the early 1990s many schools were only just beginning to introduce the National Curriculum. I did not come across many teachers who were enamoured of the government's micro-management of what was being taught in classrooms. The National Curriculum not only determines the content of what is taught but also sets attainment targets for learning and determines how performance will be assessed and reported.

Similarly, in the US many teachers and educationalists have voiced concern about the No Child Left Behind Act of 2001, which requires every US state to develop standardized assessments in maths, reading and science in order to receive federal funding for their schools. The focus of No Child Left Behind on standardized testing encourages teachers to 'teach to the test': teaching particular skills that will increase test performance rather than deepen pupils' knowledge of a broader range of subjects. The emphasis on testing in No Child Left Behind in the US, and in the National Curriculum in the UK, and the bureaucratic means proposed to raise standards were always going to get teachers' backs up.

The UK National Curriculum was first introduced under a Conservative government in the late 1980s. Since then New Labour governments have managed to make the Tory regime look relatively hands-off, by introducing one educational initiative after another that further pre-scribes how teachers should assess and test their pupils. The Association of Teachers and Lecturers has quite rightly criticized the government for its obsession with the 'three Ts' (Tests, Targets and league Tables).

At the time of writing, one of the latest in this continuous policy churn is the Early Years Foundation Stage (EYFS) framework, pub-lished in March 2007 (DfES 2007). From September 2008 every regis-tered early-years provider and school is required to follow the EYFS and monitor children's progress according to sixty-nine 'early learning goals'. Apart from embodying the notion that young children can be put on some kind of officially approved conveyor belt towards success, through meeting their sixty-nine learning goals, the EYFS framework also outlined several hundred developmental milestones against which children should be assessed. According to the document, children under the age of one should show an ability to communicate through 'crying, gurgling, babbling and squealing', and should be able to 'play with their own fingers and toes' and 'focus on objects around them'. Toddlers up to two years of age should be interested in 'putting objects in and out of containers' and should 'begin to move to music, [and] listen to or join in with rhymes or songs'.

There will be OfStEd inspections to measure child carers' perfor-mance against EYFS national standards. So we're told, for instance, that infants get a lot of enjoyment from 'finding their nose, eyes or tummy' and therefore carers should monitor whether babies are showing an interest in such games. But what if some babies don't? What conclusion should a carer draw if a child is not really interested in tummy-finding activities? No child care professional or researcher could really answer that question with any degree of certainty.

There is no convincing case for implementing such detailed monitoring of young children's behaviour and their carers' responses to that behaviour. Beverley Hughes, UK children's Minister, said, 'This government is committed to giving every child the best start in life … We know that good early-years provision leads to better outcomes in a young person's future education and life chances' (DfES 13 March 2007).

In fact, we really don't know at all whether early-years provision, whether good or bad, determines children's life chances. No serious researcher would draw such a conclusion from the studies into early-years education carried out to date. Studies investigating the short-term effect of early-years programmes on cognitive and emotional development suggest the evidence that it provides future benefits is murky at best. And there is no clear evidence at all that early-years education has longer-term benefits in terms of educational achievement and positive life or career chances in the future.

As I have argued in earlier chapters, children are unpredictable and cannot be moulded to order from birth. Indeed, one of the world's most influential developmental psychologists, Jean Piaget, has been rightly criticized by researchers in the field (including many of his followers) for trying to apply overly rigid age ranges to his proposed stages of emotional, cognitive and moral development. A century of research has given us great insights into what children should be capable of at different stages of development – but it has also taught us that children vary greatly in the pace and nature of their development. It is difficult to draw any firm conclusions from certain children's developmental delay, or to make any grand assessment of their cognitive, emotional or linguistic futures.

The targets approach to education captures governments' suspicion of teachers, who apparently cannot be left to their own devices without risking unspecific but dire consequences. The net effect is to undermine teacher autonomy and quash creativity in teaching.

Commenting on the announcement in 2006 of the two-year Primary Review, hailed as 'the first major investigation into British primary schooling since the Plowden report' of 1967, the late Steve Sinnott, then NUT General Secretary, said, 'Such a review is long overdue. The primary curriculum is overloaded and overprescriptive and wastes teaching and learning time. It is a regime that has needed major re-examination for a long time' (BBC Online 13 October 2006).

In the witness sessions for the preliminary Primary Review report entitled *Community Soundings*, teachers complained that the curriculum was 'over-structured and rigid' and 'subverted the goal of learning for its own sake' (Primary Review 2007: 23). Head teachers complained that 'bureaucratic' pressure was supplanting the 'proper task of educating children and providing educational leadership' (Primary Review 2007: 33). Indeed, educational leadership is something that is being continually eroded by government meddling in the nitty-gritty of what goes on in the classroom.

Teachers also argued that the constant testing, in the form of SATs, is 'highly stressful' to themselves as well as their pupils. Maybe so – although it is worth noting that the pupils in the Primary Review 'witness sessions', or focus groups, did not indicate they were 'stressed out' by SATs. Teachers often seem to use the 'children are stressed' line to avoid having the hard argument about the never-ending stream of government initiatives that tell them what to teach and how to relate to pupils. Unsure of how to oppose government meddling in the minutiae of their daily lives, and stand up for their professional autonomy, there is a tendency to hide behind the children, effectively saying, 'Things need to change otherwise the poor little mites will become stressed and depressed ... ' There is little doubt, however, that many teachers are pretty unhappy about many aspects of the education system today – and, in many respects, they have good cause.

At the end of *Community Soundings* the researchers list questions 'arising from this strand of the Primary Review' which they propose to take forward to the next stage of the research. The questions include:

> If, as witnesses tell us, there has been a loss in recent years of social cohesion, community and concern for others, and a growth in selfishness and materialism, how might primary schools both

help children to cope with the adverse consequences of these changes and play their part in redressing the balance?

(Primary Review 2007: 45)

Does the *Every Child Matters* agenda represent the best available way of securing children's well-being, identifying children at risk and protecting them from harm ... ? How might schools strike the best balance between protecting children from the dangers which some of them may confront outside school and overprotecting them?

(Primary Review 2007: 45 and 46)

I have a different question: Wouldn't we be better off if teachers were allowed to get on with teaching, instead of being expected to behave as social workers, psychologists, happiness counsellors, health and safety officers and police officers too?

Secondary school teacher Kevin Rooney, writing on *spiked*, has warned against this broadening of teachers' roles:

Academic subjects have become subordinate to the imperative of social engineering. The curriculum is increasingly seen principally as a vehicle for overt socialisation, even indoctrination, into the latest fashionable cause or value. No matter what the subject, teachers are now expected to make links in their schemes of work and lesson plans to topics as diverse as safe sex, relationships, healthy eating, diversity, homophobia, Islamophobia, voting, volunteering and sustainability, to list just a few.

(Rooney 29 October 2007)

And that's only the start of it. Not long after this first interim report of the Primary Review was published, Ed Balls, Secretary of State for Children, Schools and Families, launched the government's ten-year Children's Plan. The government's strategy includes giving schools 'a new role as the centre of their communities' and helping create 'more effective links between schools, the NHS and other children's services so that together they can engage parents and tackle all the barriers to the learning, health and happiness of every child' (DCSF 2007a: 3). The report states that schools should play 'a vital role in promoting physical and mental health, and emotional well-being' (DCSF 2007a: 34). Schools should also 'expand the availability of Parent Support Advisers' and offer advice to parents on parenting (DCSF 2007a: 24).

This is really not a good plan – either for teachers or for children. Teachers are increasingly lumbered with the task of looking after children's health and well-being, rather than being allowed to get on with the task of educating them. 'Schools are being seen as the vehicle for delivering a range of public policy issues, from emotional literacy to parenting, citizenship and practical financial skills', former Director of the Children's Play Council (now Play England), Tim Gill, has written in *No Fear* (Gill 2007: 13). Sociologist Frank Furedi, of the University of Kent, has also warned:

> The school curriculum has become a battleground for zealous campaigners and entrepreneurs keen to promote their message. Public health officials constantly demand more compulsory class-room discussions on healthy eating and obesity. Professionals obses-sed with young people's sex lives insist that schools introduce yet more sex education initiatives.
>
> (Furedi 2007: 1)

John Dunford, General Secretary of the Association of School and College Leaders (ASCL), rightly argues that 'schools and colleges cannot be expected to correct all the ills of society', adding, 'If schools and colleges are expected to lead on issues such as obesity, lack of parental support, antisocial behaviour and children in care, the likelihood is that education provision will suffer' (Lipsett 11 December 2007).

It seems to me that, lumbered with the task of correcting society's ills, teachers are becoming increasingly cynical about both children and parents. One of the more worrying aspects of *Community Soundings*, for instance, is what it reveals about teachers' and teaching assistants' views of parents. Apparently, many teaching assistants judged most people's parenting skills to be 'inadequate', and recommended encouraging mums and dads to take 'remedial parenting classes' (Primary Review 2007: 20). Teachers similarly raised concerns about 'low parental aspirations', 'unsettled home backgrounds', 'parents passing the socialization buck to schools', and 'parents' unwillingness or inability to provide educative experiences for their children' (Primary Review 2007: 23).

Government policies have set teachers and parents against each other. Now teachers are led to believe that they have to pick up the pieces for 'inadequate' parents and take responsibility for children's health and well-being. But how does the government propose to give schools a new role in tackling these 'barriers to the learning, health and happiness of every child'?

Happiness classes

One of New Labour's new panaceas is 'happiness classes': drafting in the US guru of positive psychology, Martin Seligman, to train British teachers. The government's Children's Plan claims, 'The Social and Emotional Aspects of Learning (SEAL) programme, which we expect the great majority of schools to be implementing by 2011, provides a whole school approach to promoting [social and emotional] skills' (DCSF 2007a: 33). Not long ago I was joking that the government would soon be introducing 'happiness' targets – only to find that it actually is proposing to do so. 'Because social and emotional skills are of such importance to unlocking children's potential, we will develop a national measure of children and young people's social and emotional skills at key transition points in their education,' the report states (DCSF 2007a: 36).

According to Richard Layard, a key government adviser on 'happiness lessons' and author of the 2005 book *Happiness: Lessons from a New Science*, we need 'an educational revolution in which a central purpose of our schools is to teach young people about the main secrets of happiness for which we have empirical evidence' (Layard May 2007). The secrets of happiness, according to Layard, include:

If you care more about other people relative to yourself, you are more likely to be happy. If you constantly compare yourself with other people, you are less likely to be happy. Choose goals that stretch you, but are attainable with high probability. Challenge your negative thoughts, and focus on the positive aspects of your character and situation.

(Layard 2007: 20)

Research published in 2006 by the Institute of Education (IoE) into the effect of the SEAL programme in primary schools purportedly shows that it is beneficial to pupils and teachers – reducing their stress levels and boosting their enthusiasm for study (Hallam *et al.* 2006). The approach, which apparently provides 'a whole school structure to deal with emotional concepts' (DCSF 2007a: 74), includes 'well-being assemblies' and curriculum materials for use in 'circle time'. Susan Hallam, author of the IoE research, said:

Most of the effort in recent years has been on academic work. SEAL gives teachers and pupils permission to think about things that are not academic. It allows them to take time to consider how they think about themselves and others.

(Borland 5 September 2007)

It should be noted that the evaluation of SEAL was based on interviews and questionnaires derived from local authority co-ordinators, head teachers, teachers, teaching assistants, children and parents. Considering that the invitation to participate in the programme depended on 'awareness of this type of approach', 'enthusiasm and commitment', 'strong leadership', and 'capacity to sustain the initiative', among other factors, could the staff's positive evaluation not be coloured by their commitment to the programme in the first place? (Hallam *et al.* 2006: 66).

In their provocatively entitled book *The Dangerous Rise of Therapeutic Education* Kathryn Ecclestone and Dennis Hayes have carried out an extensive analysis of the rise of well-being initiatives across the whole education system (Ecclestone and Hayes 2008). A key theme in their analysis is that a diverse range of arguments are being used to promote programmes such as SEAL – from the claim that it can combat the stress and anxiety of testing, and help resist the 'toxicity' of childhood itself, to the assertion that 'well-being' is as important an educational outcome as traditional subject-based knowledge and skills. Their book shows the chaotic array of concerns being piled into emotional initiatives. And on what basis?

Richard Layard claims that the 'secrets of happiness', listed above, have been 'rigorously established by modern psychology' (Layard 2007). But are we really to believe that the exploration of the human condition by great writers, artists, philosophers and, more recently, psychologists – from Shakespeare to Freud, from Leonardo da Vinci to Ernest Hemingway – over the last centuries, can be discarded for a few clichéd sound-bites about 'what makes us happy'? The worst thing is that Layard's claims are taken seriously in policy circles – indicating the philistinism of those who run the country. Just because government Ministers have swallowed 'the Science tells us' assertions about the secrets of happiness, it does not mean we should fall for such simple and formulaic answers.

What a dull world we would inhabit if every human being subscribed to Layard's happiness mottoes. A world full of such robotic beings could never have brought about fundamental changes in the world. How could our forebears have brought about great art or literature, phenomenal scientific breakthroughs or grand engineering feats if everyone in the past had chosen only 'goals that stretch [them], but are attainable with high probability'? Children should be educated about society's many great discoveries, be taught about our history and culture, be equipped with the tools to understand the physical and social world we inhabit and be taught how to appreciate great art and literature. This is the 'central purpose' of schools, not teaching young people about 'the main secrets of happiness'. Through being given the opportunity to experience a sense of achievement, develop independence of thought and a sense of autonomy, and learn through mistakes and take control of one's life, children are far more likely to feel 'happiness' whatever that state may be.

Police checks and no-touch policies

The irony is that, although teachers are increasingly given the responsibility for children's health and well-being, the government clearly does not think they can be trusted to relate to children in a healthy way without prescriptive advice and someone looking over their shoulder.

The 2007 Department for Education and Skills (DfES) document *Safeguarding Children and Safer Recruitment in Education* states:

> It is vital that local authorities, schools and FE colleges, as well as agencies that supply staff to the education sector and those that contract with the education sector to provide services that give rise to contact with children, adopt robust recruitment and vetting procedures that minimize the risk of employing people who might abuse children, or are otherwise unsuited to work with them.
>
> (DfES 2007:20)

In fact the *Building Brighter Futures* document states that 'One of Government's main roles in safeguarding the young and vulnerable is to help prevent unsuitable people from gaining access to them through their work' (DCSF 2007a: 51). It later boasts, 'Through the Safeguarding Vulnerable Groups Act 2006, we have legislated to create the most robust scheme ever for vetting individuals who are applying to work with children' (DCSF 2007: 51).

The Criminal Records Bureau (CRB) was set up after the 1997 Police Act to improve access to criminal record checks of those working with children. As Jennie Bristow wrote on *spiked* back in 2002:

> The establishment of the [CRB], the agency responsible for running these checks, was a politically motivated project, feeding off the worst New Labour mix of posturing, pragmatism and political scaremongering. Its outcome will be to fuel further distrust between parents, teachers and children, and create a climate in which those who work with children are treated with suspicion simply for doing their jobs.
>
> (Bristow 4 September 2002)

Indeed, such is the climate of suspicion surrounding adults who work with children today that teachers, youth club workers and others are reluctant to comfort injured or distressed kids. Important research carried out by Dr Heather Piper and a team at Manchester Metropolitan University showed a growing unease among teachers, and even nursery workers, about touching the children in their care (Piper *et al.* 2006). Piper reported a number of worrying incidences, including a male gym teacher leaving a girl injured in the hall while he waited for a female colleague, and a teacher refusing to put a plaster on a child's scraped knee. 'Current practice is more dependent on fears of accusation and litigation than any concern for a child,' the researchers argued (Piper *et al.* 2006: 151).

The researchers found that anxiety about touching children is mainstream. So why are those people the researchers describe as 'decent and competent childcare professionals' depriving children of the care they need? Piper believes that the staff have internalized a sense of mistrust: they have ended up watching each other for signs of suspicious behaviour. She describes this as a 'perfect panopticon'. The 'panopticon' is an 'all-seeing' type of prison, a concept invented by the philosopher Jeremy Bentham, which allows an observer to watch all prisoners without the prisoners being able to tell whether they were being observed or not. Bentham said the Panopticon was 'a new mode of obtaining power of mind over mind, in a quantity hitherto without example'.

Piper's metaphor is germane; and it helps us understand some of the behaviour of teaching staff. Teachers and teaching assistants have developed an unsettled sense of being watched, coupled with uncertainty about what is appropriate and inappropriate behaviour. As a result, their behaviour becomes stilted and unnatural. For example, Piper's team found that some of the schools that were drafting guidelines about appropriate touching consulted parents about what they thought was appropriate. One parent said: 'I would like my child to be consulted before she is touched ... I want my child to receive positive physical contact as praise – such as ruffling hair/patting on back – if that's okay with her' (Appleton 28 February 2006).

When adult behaviour is scrutinized and prescribed to this extent, spontaneous contact and interaction becomes impossible. Can this really be good for kids – or the professionals who work with them?

Scripting teachers' talk

Teachers have for some time been presented by policymakers as unthinking adults who need government advice on everything from monitoring young children's gurgling and pencil holding to how to relate to children's emotions. After the terrorist attacks of 11 September 2001 in the US, for instance, the UK government published guidelines for schools on how to help children understand the events and to cope with their aftermath. The Department for Education and Skills (DfES) warned that 'children and young people may have generalized fears triggered by the attacks, fear of further terrorist attacks or may have been upset by the images they have seen on television' (DfES 2001).

The fact was that, despite all this concern, there was a distinct lack of evidence that children were adversely affected or distressed by the events on 11 September. Rather, the preoccupation with children's emotional welfare seemed to be a case of adults projecting their own fears and insecurities on to children. A colleague's eleven-year-old brother described how his classmates discussed among themselves (in gory detail, as many adults did) what they had watched on television on 11 September: 'We were saying to each other, "Did you see those people jumping out of the windows?!"' The horror of the event didn't stop them inventing a new playground game called 'Blow up bin Laden': 'We started screaming and running every time a plane passed. We were only joking, but the teachers asked us to pray for peace and stop messing about.'

School educational psychologist Alistair Hewitt told me a few weeks after the events that he had seen no evidence that the children he dealt with were preoccupied with 11 September. Life carries on 'pretty much as normal', he said. And his own two young children 'were curious, of course, and asked loads of questions at the time – but, no, it hasn't affected them'.

Of course children are not untouched by what they see on the news, and parents and teachers had to answer some difficult questions in the weeks following 11 September. But children often see harrowing images – and they cope. Generations of children have been subjected to terrible television images – they have seen victims of war, starvation, natural disasters. An image that sticks in my mind from my childhood in Norway was when the Alexander Kielland accommodation platform sank in the North Sea in 1980 when one of its five columns broke off in a storm – killing 123 people on board. I still remember the look of horror and grief on the faces of adults when the names of all the young men killed were listed on television.

Some images and events make a lasting impression on children. But children's reactions to terrible images are formed more by the reactions of the adults around them than by the images themselves. So surely what was most damaging to children post-11 September was not the actual television images but adults' responses. As Jay Mathews pointed out in the *Washington Post* on the huge number of holiday cancellations post-11 September: 'What young people will learn from the decision to cancel their travel plans is "when bad things happen, hide under the rug"' (Mathews 2 October 2001).

The DfES admitted that 'teachers, who know their own pupils, are most likely to recognize any uncharacteristic behaviour and are best placed to decide how to deal with them' – but it still felt compelled to issue its guidelines on helping children cope with the images (DfES 2001). And teachers' trade unions, local authorities, psychiatric and counselling institutions on both sides of the Atlantic bombarded teachers with official advice about helping children cope after 11 September. Why?

According to the DfES, the demand came from teachers themselves, who apparently were desperately seeking advice on how to help children who might be traumatized. But it is hardly surprising – when just about every aspect of the teacher's day is prescribed by the government – that teachers feel impotent to use their own know-how and nous. This is one of the biggest problems with the plethora of advice being offered to teachers today. Constant 'expert advice' on how to relate to children is ultimately disabling, stripping adults of common sense and teaching teachers not to cope on their own.

Much of the guidance issued in relation to 11 September was plain common sense – and therefore unnecessary. Experts recommended again and again that information given to children should be 'age appropriate, handled gently, and explained in terms children understand'. I think teachers could work that out for themselves. But the National Union of Teachers (NUT) was not so sure – its web site advised: 'In responding to pupils' need for explanation of the events, teachers should assess pupils' level of understanding and emotional maturity, prior to deciding on how much information is appropriate' (NUT 2001). Similarly the American Academy of Child and Adolescent Psychiatry (AACAP) advised: 'It is important to explain the event in words the child can understand' (AACAP 2004). And on the resource page for parents and teachers on 'How to Talk to Children about the Threat of Biological Warfare or Terrorist Attack' the US Federal Emergency Management Agency (FEMA) recommended: 'We need to keep in mind that when kids ask questions about dangers and risks, they are usually looking for a little bit of two things – understandable information and realistic reassurance' (FEMA 2001).

The reality is, one cannot and should not prescribe how to communicate with children. There is no 'correct' script. Those best placed to answer tough questions are not anonymous 'experts' from outside but teachers and parents who know, care for, and understand the children in their charge.

TEN

LET STRANGERS BE FRIENDS

How the 'stranger danger' panic is creating a
hostile adult world

*The vast majority of adults do not intend to harm children they do not
know. So strangers are a largely dependable source of help if things go
wrong.*

(Tim Gill, 2007, p. 53)

In an episode of the popular US television series *Crime Scene
Investigation* (*CSI*) one of the investigators, Catherine Willows, con-
fides to her boss, Gil Grissom, her concerns about her twelve-year-old
daughter. Willows's daughter, going through a rebellious phase after
the death of her father, thinks she can do as she pleases – even hitch-
hiking into town. Grissom sombrely asks Willows whether she has
told her daughter about the dangers of the adult world – meaningfully
turning his gaze to the room where a post-mortem is being carried out
on the body of a young girl. The *CSI* team are in the middle of investigating the death of a schoolgirl whose body has been found wrapped
in a bloody blanket in a remote field on the outskirts of Las Vegas. The
girl is presumed to have been murdered by a known paedophile (although
it later emerges that it was her own brother who took her life).

Willows is reluctant to tell her daughter about all the daily horrors
they come across in their line of work, she tells Grissom, 'because

I don't want to scare my daughter into growing up fearing life'. Having been told by Grissom that there is a difference between *scaring* children about the world and *preparing* them for the world, Willows inexplicably takes her young daughter down to the mortuary, opens the door of one of the chambers and pulls out the body of a young girl. Forcing her daughter to look at the dead girl's battered face, she asks, 'Now do you understand why I won't let you hitch-hike?'

Thank God it's fiction. The vast majority of real-life adults are rather more sensible and sensitive. But not many children will be immune to the drip-drip effect of continual – and often barely more subtle – warnings about the risks they face in the outside world.

The *Times* (London) raised an interesting question during 2007's Playday: 'How many people does it take to give a child a taste of what it's like to play in the streets, just as they did in the old days?' The answer was:

> Their parents, of course, allowing them out on the occasion of the national Playday this week, part of a campaign for more freedom for our closeted kids to romp outdoors. But, at one of the sites, a small residential street in Aldershot, it also required five policemen, three community support officers, a traffic management crew, a CC-TV van and a team of 'play workers' from the local council.
>
> (Miles and Rumbelow 4 August 2007)

Why all the supervision? According to one of the child care development workers involved, a police presence is necessary because 'there are lots of alleyways and hedges'. The event had been advertised locally, so there was concern about it attracting paedophiles and abductors. What kind of message does this mistrustful better-safe-than-sorry attitude give to parents and children?

In this climate, it is little wonder that parents do not feel confident letting their children play unsupervised in the streets and local parks. Particularly when it is assumed by many that any parents who do let

their child out and about on their own are bad parents. As Simon
Knight, a senior community worker for a Scottish local authority and
a director of Generation Youth Issues, told me:

> This is the basis on which much government policy is founded …
> Almost all state-sponsored youth work today is about getting
> children off the streets. Isn't it ironic? In the name of combating
> antisocial behaviour people, in jobs much like my own, are
> charged with acting like the Child Catcher in *Chitty Chitty Bang
> Bang* and tasked with clearing children off the streets – the very
> place where they learn to be social in the first place.

Some local authorities and police forces have even adopted the con-
troversial 'Mosquito' – a device that gives off a high-pitched noise
audible only to those under twenty years of age. Its purpose is to
disperse youth and force them away from shopping centres and other
public areas. There are an estimated 3,500 Mosquitoes used across the
UK. So, on one hand, youth workers are tasked with clearing kids
from public spaces, some with the aid of Orwellian devices such as
the Mosquito; on the other, parents are chastised for not letting their
children go out in public on their own. This says a lot about the
screwed-up approach to children today.

Worryingly, research indicates that children are internalizing many
adult fears and insecurities. A study carried out by the think-tank Demos
and the environmental group Green Alliance entitled *A Child's Place*
shows that children would like to spend more time out of the house
but are often too frightened to do so (Thomas and Thompson 2004).
Interviewing over 1,000 ten and eleven-year-olds, they found that the
deciding factor in the children's preference for particular environments
was whether they saw it as safe or not. The dangers the children worried
about most in relation to spending time in public spaces were: traffic,
strangers, getting lost, bullying and vandalism, trains and, finally,
terrorism. (The Madrid bombings took place during the field study.)

It is understandable that children worry about traffic, as roads are
dangerous places, and children need to appreciate that cars can kill in

order to appreciate the need for road sense. But that a fear of strangers looms so large in children's imagination has a much weaker basis in reality. The Demos researchers found that the garden was the only outdoor space a large number of children felt was safe from strangers. One girl from Wick said, 'I feel most comfortable in the garden. Because I know that there's no strangers there, and no one can get me or anything' (Thomas and Thompson 2004: 8).

We wouldn't want children to grow up naive to the dangers of the world, but do we really want the current generation growing up fearing for their own safety outside the confines of their own homes? Do we want children to see every adult they do not know as a potential threat?

Some months ago I was getting out of a car just outside a friend's house in Balsall Heath in Birmingham. There was a group of children, between eight and ten years of age, playing on the pavement on either side of the street next to parked cars. They were engrossed in play. I caught one of the girls' eye as I was getting out of the car. 'Hello there!' she shouted and gave me a large cheeky grin. She had never met me before. 'Hello,' I smiled back. To me it seemed rather unusual, though heartening, to see children having fun outside with no parents in sight. Also, it is a rare occurrence to come across children who have no compunction about talking to strangers. Of course, the young girl may have felt emboldened by being surrounded by her siblings and friends. But she clearly had not completely taken to heart today's motto 'Never speak to strangers.'

As a child I remember being given specific instructions about never to get into strangers' cars, and being particularly wary of strange men offering sweets in return for following them somewhere. Not that we knew of anybody this had happened to, but we took the stern and specific warning to heart. Other than that, we would expect adults – whether we knew them or not – to be there for us, and help out, if we ever got into trouble. Also, we would expect them to discipline us if we misbehaved.

Inculcating children with a fear of *all* strangers is counterproductive. As Tim Gill argues in *No Fear*, telling children to 'never speak to strangers' can lead them to believe it is wrong for adults to initiate social contact with children. At a time when adult motives are treated so suspiciously it is heartening to read Gill's defence of human compassion: 'The vast majority of adults do not intend to harm children they do not know. So strangers are a largely dependable source of help if things go wrong' (Gill 2007: 53).

Today a very different image of adults is presented to children. The UK government in effect presents every adult as a potential paedophile. The Safeguarding Vulnerable Groups Act, which passed into law in England and Wales in 2006, requires millions of adults whose work involves coming into contact with children to undergo Criminal Record Bureau checks. The message this imparts to parents and children is to be suspicious of any adult who wants to work with children. Josie Appleton, who runs the Manifesto Club's campaign against the blanket vetting of all adults, argues:

> The vetting of adults in the name of child protection is out of control. Those now being vetted include sixteen-year-olds teaching younger kids to read, parents volunteering at school, and foster carers' friends. Running an after-school club is now subject to more stringent security tests than selling explosives.
>
> (Appleton 2006: 8)

Brendan O'Neill, editor of the web site *spiked*, wrote in the *Catholic Herald*:

> In the small Catholic community in north London where I grew up, there was a lot of truth to the irritating, sugary old proverb: 'It takes a village to raise a child' … Of course our mums and dads did most of the raising. But they also entrusted us to other adults … On Saturday mornings we were charged to the husband-and-wife team who, heaven help them, tried to teach us country dancing. Sometimes they even got physical with us, bending our legs and forcing our arms still against our bodies.
>
> (O'Neill 27 October 2006)

Today parents are discouraged from entrusting their children with other adults. It is a crime to work with children without first getting a criminal record check. O'Neill rightly concludes, 'this Stalinist mass monitoring of adult workers teaches children to be wary of adults' (O'Neill 27 October 2006).

The encouragement of suspicion towards adults, and attempts to insulate children from contact with strangers, could hinder the development of trusting relationships with other people. As adults we need to deal with both antagonistic and hostile, and well intentioned and sympathetic, strangers. If children have had no practice in living – simply being told to 'yell, run and tell', for instance, if approached by a stranger – how are they going to learn to read later in life the intentions of people they do not know?

Tim Gill similarly warns that the attempt to regulate contact between adults and children 'can undermine the very bonds of mutual trust that make communities welcoming, safe places for children' (Gill 2007: 48). It is an insidious message that is being put across – don't trust any adult unless they have been checked out by the police. Of course, parents and children cannot take this message to heart completely, otherwise they would not be able to get on with their everyday lives. I doubt there are many adults or children who seriously look upon every other adult in their midst as potential paedophiles. But the suspicion is more likely to be there today, under the surface, and governments – along with just about every institution and corporation – are doing a good job of fostering and feeding it.

Ian, a former colleague of mine and the father of three young children, recounted an upsetting incident on a flight from New York. At the check-in desk, with a sizeable queue behind him, he asked if he could have the 'door seat' – the row by the emergency exit – so that he would have lots of leg room. He was also hoping to 'lie on the floor to have a kip'. The check-in person said, 'Of course,' and booked him in. 'But after some more clickety-clicks she said she was sorry but that she couldn't let me have the seat after all,' Ian told me, adding, 'I asked why not – conversationally, really, since I hadn't expected to luck out on a crowded cattle class.' Her answer was that there was an 'unaccompanied minor' in one of the seats. 'That's OK, I don't mind,' said Ian, misunderstanding her point. Rather loudly the check-in person announced that he had no choice in the matter, as the airline's policy was not to seat males next to unaccompanied minors. 'I was embarrassed and cross,' said Ian: not least by 'the implication that I and all other men are paedophiles.'

Yet in our fearful times we can all be caught in the web of suspicion, being viewed as potential paedophiles. In a notorious case in 1995 the UK newsreader Julia Somerville and her boyfriend were arrested for taking snapshots of her young daughter naked in the bath. The Protection of Children Act 1978 made it a criminal offence to take indecent photographs of children. Clearly, to some people 'indecent' means naked. A photo lab. assistant at the Boot's, the pharmacy chain, reported Somerville's film to his supervisors, in line with the company's guidelines, because it contained twenty-eight shots of Somerville's daughter during bathtime. The reaction that greeted this incident revealed widespread concern among the public that the kind of photos that have traditionally appeared in any family album should now be treated as potential child pornography.

But the overblown suspicion of photographs has become far more intense in the decade following the Somerville incident. Today it is almost impossible in the UK to take photos of one's children, grand-children, nieces or nephews in public places – if they are surrounded by other children – whether or not they are naked. When my oldest nephew, Marcus, celebrated his fourth birthday with a pool party in Bristol back in 1996 I was able to take a number of shots of the children having fun in the pool. Ten years later, when his younger brother, Stefan, asked me to come and watch him during his swimming lesson and take some photos of him, all hell broke loose. Sitting by the side of the pool engrossed in conversation with a friend, I absentmindedly pulled the camera out of my bag. Mid-conversation I became aware of a kerfuffle going on in the background – whistles were being blown and lifeguards were waving their hands and shouting at someone. Turning our attention to the noise, wondering what on earth was going on, we realized that the lifeguards were shouting at *me* to put the camera away, as if I had taken a deadly weapon out of my bag. No photos could be taken of my nephew Stefan on the proud day he was able to swim an entire length of the pool for the first time.

Rules governing the use of cameras and camera-phones in swimming pools, parks, children's parties, pantomimes, school sports days and anywhere at all where children might be are now ubiquitous, and strictly enforced. One friend tells how, after her daughter celebrated her second birthday at the nursery she attended, she requested photographs of the occasion. The nursery replied that it had to seek permission from every parent of every child that appeared in the photograph: a laborious process that, perhaps not surprisingly, meant that the photographs never materialized. Another friend, who has been lucky enough to receive photos from her children's nursery about their birthday celebrations, was bemused to find that when other children appeared in the photographs their faces were scrubbed out with pen.

This heightened suspicion about images of other people's children is a curious thing. If pressed, would any nursery manager, schoolteacher or parent really think that any danger could come to a child by other parents looking at photos of the child? Instead, fantastical justifications tend to be provided, in the form of photos 'falling into the wrong hands' and ending up being appropriated by paedophile rings or published on child pornography web sites. The backdrop to these blanket prohibitions is not specific threats, let alone likely ones: rather, a general mistrust of the myriad dangers that are seen to lurk in the adult world at large.

When my nephew, at that time aged seven, was taking part in a sponsored maths test for the National Society for the Prevention of Cruelty to Children (NSPCC) – arranged by the school – in order to raise awareness of child abuse, his grandmother was quite troubled. 'I don't like it,' she told my sister. 'I think it's terrible that they're filling children's heads with all that stuff. Stefan's such an innocent boy and so fun-loving. Why do they want to fill his head with these nasty things?' Having thought the same myself, I was glad that she had raised her concern. We both agreed we would sponsor Stefan, as he was so motivated to do the maths challenge, but we would make it clear to him that we did not agree with the campaign, and why.

Looking into the NSPCC's 'Don't hide it' campaign – unfortunately, after having handed over the money – I found it is more sinister than I first suspected. Launching the high-profile campaign, which they urged schools to teach their pupils about, NSPCC director Mary Marsh said, 'A child calls ChildLine on average once every hour to talk about rape and other types of sexual abuse' (NSPCC 15 May 2006). She added, 'Children have phoned in to talk in confidence about having been raped in toilets, phone boxes, cars, bedrooms, bushes, parks and elsewhere.' The NSPCC claims that research shows one in six children will be sexually abused before they reach their sixteenth birthday, but nearly three-quarters (72 per cent) tell no one about it at the time. Why, indeed, would a charity that cares about children want to 'fill their heads' with the notion that they, or their friends, are likely to fall victim to sexual abuse?

Fortunately, children are rather less susceptible than the NSPCC to believing the bad in everybody. Several months after Stefan had collected the sponsorship money I phoned him up to find out what he had taken on board from the NSPCC's visit. I asked him if he could remember what it was he was raising money for when he did the maths challenge. 'Yes,' he said confidently, 'the NSPCC.' 'I see,' I said, 'and what did they need money for?' 'They look after children whose parents are cruel to them,' he answered, 'and they pay for play areas and toys for the children.' What Stefan took on board from the NSPCC's visit was maybe not that different from what children would have taken on board from fairy stories in the past – like the wicked witch who imprisoned Hansel and Gretel, or Cinderella's evil stepmother. Children will deduce that some adults can be really evil. Stefan's appreciation that indeed there are some people in the world who are excessively cruel does not necessarily shape how he views the adults he comes into contact with on a daily basis.

It would be wrong to assume that children unquestioningly internalize today's miserablist culture. I doubt an entire generation is going to turn into complete cynics always suspecting the basest of motives in the behaviour of fellow human beings. For a start, most children's everyday experience does not correspond with the messages they are given about adults. Adults are, on the whole, compassionate and caring rather than cruel and abusing. But I still worry about the drip-drip effect of today's misanthropic culture. One way or another, children will pick up signals about stranger danger, the problem of photography, the implications of vetting – and the only message it is possible to draw from this is that it should not be taken for granted that you can trust adults.

Walk on by

Another side effect of today's culture of fear – and in particular of the paedophile panic – is that adults no longer feel confident to step in to help children in trouble. Neither do many adults, particularly in the UK, feel they can discipline other people's children if they are misbehaving. As Frank Furedi told me when his book *Paranoid Parenting* came out in 2001, his key concern was 'the breakdown of adult solidarity':

> Being an adult does not simply mean being biologically mature or chronologically grown-up. Above all, it should mean having a certain sense of responsibility towards non-adults: recognising the need to have a nurturing and guiding relationship to the younger generation.

Adults seem to have lost that sense, argues Furedi:

> They don't tend to stop and help children if they are in trouble. They don't discipline children who are misbehaving ... or help out parents by looking after their children as a matter of course.

Adult solidarity is not a radically new idea – especially when you consider that 'across cultures, and throughout history, mothers and fathers have acted on the assumption that if their children got into trouble other adults – often strangers – would help out', as Furedi explains. But, for obvious reasons, it was greeted with 'a sharp intake of breath and a strong sense of defensiveness' by the parenting industry – the experts at the sharp end of Furedi's critique. To them the idea that parents should rely on the general public to help them out rather than highly trained government-approved 'experts' like themselves sounds entirely alien and highly dodgy.

A few years ago I was in a park with my nephews when I saw a young girl stuck on the top of a climbing frame, whimpering with fear. There were no adults in sight. Although I felt a little uneasy about helping her down, particularly since the girl had a short dress on, I would have felt a lot uneasier if I had not had my young nephews with me. How would a lone male have felt about stepping in to help? Would he have turned the other way for fear of being suspected of having sinister motives? A survey of 500 men by Identikids, the ID tag company, found that 75 per cent of men will not help children in distress for fear of what it looks like to others. Because of heightened awareness of paedophilia there is concern about helping children in public places who appear to be lost or in a vulnerable situation. Twenty-three per cent would ignore the child completely. Others would find a woman or another member of the public. This suspicion extends to other adults too: 67 per cent of men would be concerned about the intent of a man who did approach a distressed child.

This is not just a UK phenomenon. Canadian therapist Michael Ungar writes in *Too Safe for Their own Good*:

> I'm always anxious about helping a child who isn't mine in public places. I'm always worried about what parents will think. What will they make of a strange man touching their child even if it is only in the most innocent of ways? I hear other parents say they too are no longer willing to take responsibility for the unsupervised children in our communities.
>
> (Ungar 2007: 64)

In the summer of 2007 Jeffrey Zaslow wrote an article in the *Wall Street Journal* about how our culture teaches children to fear men in particular (Zaslow 23 August 2007). He was inundated with letters from men lamenting this growing suspicion of adult males and admitting that they had in turn become fearful of children: 'They said they avert their eyes when kids are around, or think twice before holding even their own children's hands in public' (Zaslow 6 September 2007). It is a sad state of affairs when the suspicion goes so far that some US child advocates advise parents never to hire male babysitters.

It may be true that males are more likely than females to sexually abuse children. Ninety-eight per cent of the volunteers who have faced allegations of abuse while working with the US youth mentoring organization Big Brothers Big Sisters are male. But there are only a handful of abuse allegations a year out of hundreds of thousands of volunteers: and not all allegations are true. Mack Koonce, the group's chief operating officer, points out: 'If we wanted to make sure we never had a problem, one approach would be to just become Big Sisters – to say we won't serve boys' (Zaslow 6 September 2007). But, as Zaslow writes, 'of course, that would deny hundreds of thousands of boys contact with male mentors'.

That could happen unless we start countering today's suspicion of adults – and adult males in particular. A survey of more than 1,000 people by Scotland's Commissioner for Children and Young People in October 2007 revealed that males are often too scared of being branded a paedophile to work with young people (BBC Online 16 October 2007). They described the prospect of being falsely accused of abusing a child as 'the worst thing imaginable' – which it probably is. Being suspected of sexually abusing children is likely to tear one's life apart. Forty-eight per cent of adults surveyed said this fear was a barrier to contact with children and young people generally, and this same fear also made them much less likely to help when seeing a young person in danger or distress.

The way forward

So what is the way forward? It is not easy for parents to go against the grain and give their children more freedom than today's society deems acceptable.

Hilde, a friend of my sister's, was in London with her two young children on a visit from Norway. Returning from a trip to the local park, Hilde found that her youngest child, Buster, had fallen asleep in the pushchair. As is customary in Norway, she left him napping in the buggy outside the front door of my sister's house, on a fairly quiet street in leafy East Dulwich. But, much to Hilde's astonishment, within a few minutes there was an impatient knock at the door. An extremely agitated passer-by wanted to know whether Hilde was the mother of the 'abandoned' child in the buggy. When Hilde confirmed that she was indeed the mother of the child, who was not abandoned but merely left to sleep in peace, the passer-by threatened to call the police and the social services to report Hilde's 'irresponsible' behaviour. Hilde was too outraged by the woman's manner to defuse the situation. However, after a lot of gentle persuasion from Hilde's partner, the woman relented and agreed to 'let the matter pass ... this time!'

There may not be many people who would go to the lengths of threatening to involve the police and the social services when they believe parents are not keeping a sufficiently watchful eye on their children. However, most parents will be aware that they are likely to get disapproving looks, or hurtful comments behind their backs, if they leave their children in situations where potentially they could come to some harm – however remote the chances.

In April 2008 the *New York Sun* columnist Lenore Skenazy wrote an article entitled 'Why I let my nine-year-old ride the subway alone' (Skenazy 1 April 2008). She gave her son a subway map, a MetroCard, a $20 bill and several quarters, 'just in case he had to make a call', waved him bye-bye and told him she'd see him at home. She wrote:

> I trusted him to figure out that he should take the Lexington Avenue subway down, and the Thirty-fourth Street cross-town bus home. If he couldn't do that, I trusted him to ask a stranger. And then I even trusted that stranger not to think, 'Gee, I was about to catch my train home, but now I think I'll abduct this adorable child instead.'
>
> (Skenazy 1 April 2008)

Skenazy later described in the *Times* (London) how she suddenly became 'a lightning rod in the parenting wars' (Skenazy 9 June 2008). 'Mention my story, and millions of people not only know about it, they have a very strong opinion about it, and me, and my parenting skills – or utter, shameful lack thereof.' She described how she became branded 'America's worst mom' simply for allowing her child to do what most people her age had done routinely when they were his age. But there were also many parents who applauded her decision to let her son travel alone.

In response to an article I wrote on how children's lives are restricted by today's safety-obsessed culture (Guldberg 2007) I received a number of interesting e-mails from concerned parents. Valerie, a mother in her forties with two young children, wrote from Canada:

> I figured that the time I would have to spend arranging for my son to play with his friends (and supervising them) would decrease as he got older, because he would be perfectly capable of going to their house. He just started at a new preschool which functions as a feeder to his elementary school and all of his classmates live within walking or biking distance. They would be perfectly capable of coming to ours [or] somebody else's house, just like I did when I was a kid. But apparently that is no longer [acceptable]. I don't agree with this but anybody else I speak to has accepted it as the norm, even if they don't really agree with it either. I don't think anybody around here would say they live in an unsafe neighborhood. And yet they all act as if they do ... Mothers are condemning themselves to more of a hands-on role than I really think we need to play or want to play for that matter.

As I have argued in previous chapters, parents need to give children more freedom to roam and mess about – even if they may end up in some difficult situations. The rather pejorative term 'helicopter parents' is increasingly used to describe parents who 'hover' over their children at all times. But it is not good enough pointing the finger at parents and telling them to 'get a grip' or 'chill a little more'.

Nor is it good enough to pin all the blame on the media. Of course, the media have a lot to answer for. No doubt parental fears have been exacerbated by the relentless reporting of the disappearance of Madeleine McCann in 2007, and the previous stories we remember only too well: the murders of Soham schoolgirls Holly Wells and Jessica Chapman in 2002, and the abduction and killing of Sarah Payne in 2000; the US coverage of the abduction, rape and murder of eleven-year-old Carlie Brucia in 2004 and seven-year-old Megan Kanka in 1994. Alongside this, journalists and reporters constantly tell us how dangerous the modern world is for children, and unquestionably cover the advocacy research that backs up this doom-mongering world view. Hardly a day goes by without new media reports suggesting that children and young people are on the verge of a mental breakdown, at risk from paedophiles, bullying, antisocial behaviour, drugs and alcohol, and are facing an obesity epidemic that will result in them 'dying before their parents'. All this no doubt contributes to a sense that the world is a scary and threatening place for kids.

But to focus all our fire on media scaremongering, as many critics of today's safety-obsessed culture often do, is to let more official sources of fear off the hook: in particular, governments, and the charities they create and sponsor. For example, in the UK, it was a report published by the House of Commons Health Select Committee in 2004 that triggered the irrational panic about the obesity epidemic that would apparently 'kill off' many of our children; it is the government's Sex Offenders Register that institutionalizes the idea that perverted adults are stalking kids; it is the government's Safeguarding Vulnerable Groups Act, a piece of legislation that legitimates spying on millions of adults, which communicates the message 'Children are at risk – from everyone'. And numerous charities, including the NSPCC and ChildLine, help to sustain the idea that life is worse for children than in the past.

Even those parents who against the grain try to give their children more freedom than is considered normal today cannot be immune to the constant reminders of the dreadful things that can happen. As

Mick Hume, editor-at-large of *spiked*, wrote in June 2007, the sixth week of the coverage of the abduction of Madeleine McCann, 'If one child abduction story fades, we can be sure that another horror tale about paedophiles will be along soon, bringing with it the ghosts of previous cases' (Hume 14 June 2007).

On the same day front pages of the UK press led with headlines declaring 'Paedos to be chemically castrated'. This was in response to an announcement by then Home Secretary, John Reid, that the government aimed to crack down on child sex abuse by introducing voluntary drug treatments to curb the sex drive of offenders and bring in laws allowing single mothers to check whether their new boyfriend was a convicted paedophile. Mick Hume noted:

> New Labour has also pledged a new 'paedophile awareness campaign', as if it were possible to raise public 'awareness' of this issue any higher. The campaign will, in the words of one report, 'hammer home the grim message that 90 per cent of child abuse is carried out by people the victims know'. In other words, the government wants us to be more 'aware' (or perhaps just beware) that 'stranger danger' is the least of our worries, and that any parent or loved one could be a pervert and a paedophile, too.
>
> (Hume 14 June 2007)

Those of us concerned about this culture of mistrust should challenge the various government-driven and media-fuelled campaigns that undermine trust in fellow human beings. Ultimately parents will give children the independence they need only if they have sufficient trust in other adults – trust in them not harming but looking out for other people's children. When we grew up our parents assumed that, if we got into trouble, other adults – often strangers – would help out. Today that trust does not exist – or, at least, is seriously damaged.

Adrian Voce, Director of Play England, points out:

> In the 1940s, 50s, 60s, the streets were filled with children playing and adults watching over them and joining in. Now there isn't

that community oversight of street space, so it doesn't feel that safe for children any longer.

(Miles and Rumbelow 2007)

This is not just a UK phenomenon. Paula Fass, Professor of History at the University of California, Berkeley, and author of the 2006 book *Children of a New World*, told me:

[W]hat began in the early twentieth century as a broad commitment to children as a social obligation has become in the twenty-first century much narrower gauged focus on the parents' need to guard and control their own children ... The social investment in children as a shared enterprise is in serious decline.

Adults relate less and less to children other than their own – whether that be to help them out or to discipline them. Children, of course, are sussed enough to know that they are unlikely to face sanctions from adults other than their parents and teachers. The IPPR's report *Freedom's Orphans: Raising Youth in a Changing World*, based on comparative interviews with adults in a number of European countries, found that whereas in Germany, Spain and Italy over half the respondents said they would intervene if they saw a group of four-teen-year-olds vandalizing a bus shelter, in the UK only 34 per cent said they would do something (IPPR 2006).

The lesson Frank Furedi would draw from the report is to stop pointing the finger at the bad behaviour of teenagers:

What is really distinct about Britain today is not the behaviour of youngsters but the behaviour of adults. The problem is the inability of adults to take responsibility for guiding and socialising children. Men and women rarely interact with children other than their own, often feeling too awkward to intervene when children misbehave and too confused to give support to those who are in trouble. A long time before they become teenagers, children sense and know that they face no sanctions from any adult other than their parents.

(Furedi 9 November 2006)

Adults should behave like adults and build up children's confidence to get by in the wider world. That means leading children down the road to adulthood, giving them the chance to engage with people they do not know, and giving them something to aspire to, not teaching them to fear and deride the adult world.

If we can harness a more positive outlook about our fellow human beings and challenge institutionalized suspicion and state-authorized scaremongering, then we really might free up our children's lives and allow them both to enjoy themselves and to learn through living.

AFTERWORD

I decided to write *Reclaiming Childhood* because of my concern about the extent to which society's desire to protect children from the realities of life is restricting their chances, not only to make the most of their childhood, but to grow up into capable, confident adults. By cocooning children, over-protecting and over-supervising them, society does children no favours. It is the responsibility of adults to prepare children for a full and independent life, not to protect them from every conceivable risk in the wider world.

However, the more I explored how children's lives have changed the more I recognized that children's lives have also improved in very many ways over the last century. Children are healthier and wealthier than ever before; they are given time, attention, protection and education. The crisis of childhood is caused less by the realities of the modern world than by an overly negative *perception* of the modern world which recasts opportunities as new problems and sees something suspicious in the noblest of human motivations.

The root of the problem children face today stems from the extent to which adults' motivations are automatically treated with suspicion. This has led to a breakdown of trust. Parents are not encouraged to rely on other adults to look out for their children. Instead they are encouraged to insulate their children from contact with all but a small, carefully regulated network of family, friends and child care professionals. This narrows children's world as surely as it narrows adults' minds, transforming other adults from a crucial source of trust and solidarity into a predatory spectre.

Throughout *Reclaiming Childhood* I have offered suggestions about ways that we could work to improve children's experience, and that of parents, teachers and 'strangers', simply by taking a step back from the panics and doom-mongering and trusting adults to care for the children with whom they interact. Most adults are compassionate and caring rather than cruel and abusing, and we need to get real about that.

We also need to have more faith in children. The fact that adolescents are still pushing against adult boundaries and striving towards becoming adults themselves indicates that children have not internalized all the negative messages they are getting about the world they live in and the people who live in it.

Rather than projecting fears and uncertainties on to children, adults need to allow children to grow and flourish, balancing sensible guidance with youthful independence. This means that we need to chill out a little: allowing children to play, experiment and mess around, without adults hovering over them, and giving them the opportunity to get themselves out of difficulties they may get themselves into and to resolve their own conflicts. But children cannot raise themselves. We need to guide children along the road to adulthood, by creating sensible boundaries and giving them manageable challenges. By behaving a bit more like confident, competent grown-ups we can help to give children their childhood back – and reclaim adulthood, too, as something to aspire to rather than fear.

BIBLIOGRAPHY

AACAP (American Academy of Child and Adolescent Psychiatry) (updated July 2004) *Helping Children after a Disaster*, Facts for Families No. 36, Washington DC: AACAP. Online. Available HTTP: http://aacap.org/page.ww?name=Helping+Children+After+a+Disaster&section=Facts+for+Families (accessed 3 April 2008).

Abbs, P., *et al.* (17 September 2007) 'Let our children play', London: *Daily Telegraph*. Online. Available www.telegraph.co.uk/opinion/main.jhtml?xml=/opinion/2007/09/10/nosplit/dt1001.xml (accessed 3 April 2008).

Abbs, P., *et al.* (13 September 2006) 'Modern life leads to more depression among children', London: *Daily Telegraph*. Online. Available www.telegraph.co.uk/news/main.jhtml?xml=/news/2006/09/12/nosplit/njunk112.xml (accessed 10 April 2008).

Ainsworth, M. D. S., Blehar, M. C., Waters, E., and Wall, S. (1978) *Patterns of Attachment: A Psychological Study of the Strange Situation*, Hillsdale NJ: Erlbaum.

Anderegg, D. (2003) *Worried all the Time: Rediscovering the Joy in Parenthood in an Age of Anxiety*, New York: Free Press.

Anti-Bullying Alliance (2006) *e-bulletin* 6, London: National Children's Bureau.

Appleton, J. (28 February 2006) 'Don't touch those kids!' London: Spiked. Online. Available HTTP: http://www.spiked-online.com/Articles/0000000CAF9E.htm (accessed 10 April 2008).

Appleton, J. (2006) *The Case against Vetting: How the Child Protection Industry is Poisoning Adult–Child Relations*, London: Manifesto Club. Online. Available HTTP: http://www.manifestoclub.com (accessed 10 April 2008).

Arens, U. (28 January 2006) Speech at the launch of the *Sense about Science* report 'Making Sense of Chemical Stories'.

Aries, P. (1973) *Centuries of Childhood: A Social History of Family Life*, Harmondsworth: Penguin.

Auerbach, S. (1998) *Smart Play, Smart Toys: How to Raise a Child with a High PQ*, New York: St Martin's Press.

Bailey, D., *et al.* (2001) *Critical Thinking about Critical Periods*, Baltimore MD: Brookes Publishing.

Ball, D. (2002) *Playgrounds: Risks, Benefits and Choices*, Contract Research Report 426, Sudbury: Health and Safety Executive.

Balls, E. (23 July 2007) 'Every Child Matters', speech to the National Children's Bureau at the launch of *Staying Safe*.

Basham, P., and Luik, J. (2006) *Diet Nation: Exposing the Obesity Crusade*, London: Social Affairs Unit.

Basham, P., and Luik, J. (27 November 2006) 'Four big, fat myths', London: *Sunday Telegraph*. Online. Available HTTP: http://www.telegraph.co.uk/news/main.jhtml?xml=/news/2006/11/26/nfat26.xml (accessed 3 April 2008).

BBC Online (29 December 2007) 'Toy weapons "help boys to learn"', London: BBC Online. Online. Available HTTP: http://news.bbc.co.uk/1/hi/education/7163741.stm (accessed 28 April 2008).

BBC Online (9 December 2007) 'Ads' impact on children probed', London: BBC Online. Online. Available HTTP: http://news.bbc.co.uk/1/hi/education/7134943.stm (accessed 28 April 2008).

BBC Online (16 October 2007) 'Adults "to afraid" of youth work', London: BBC Online. Online. Available HTTP: http://news.bbc.co.uk/1/hi/scotland/7045544.stm (accessed 28 August, 2008).

BBC Online (23 July 2007) 'Child depression drug use soars', London: BBC Online. Online. Available HTTP: http://news.bbc.co.uk/1/hi/health/6911596.stm (accessed 28 April 2008).

BBC Online (5 June 2007) 'Young "not allowed out to play"', London: BBC Online. Online. Available HTTP: http://news.bbc.co.uk/1/hi/education/6720231.stm (accessed 28 April 2008).

BBC Online (14 February 2007) 'UK is accused of failing children', London: BBC Online. Online. Available HTTP: http://news.bbc.co.uk/1/hi/uk/6359363.stm (accessed 10 April 2008).

BBC Online (2 November 2006) 'UK youths "among worst in Europe"', London: BBC Online. Online. Available HTTP: http://news.bbc.co.uk/1/hi/uk/6108302.stm (accessed 28 August, 2008).

BBC Online (13 October 2006) 'Fresh look at primary schooling', London: BBC Online. Online. Available HTTP: http://news.bbc.co.uk/1/hi/education/6047106.stm (accessed 15 May 2008).

BBC Online (25 July 2006) 'Government acts on cyber-bullies', London: BBC Online. Online. Available HTTP: http://news.bbc.co.uk/1/hi/education/52108 86.stm (accessed 15 May 2008).

BBC Online (20 June 2003) 'Child mental health ills "rife"', London: BBC Online. Online. Available HTTP: http://news.bbc.co.uk/1/hi/health/6221240. stm (accessed 10 April 2008).

BBC Online (10 February 2003) 'Poor mental health widespread in young', London: BBC Online. Online. Available HTTP: http://news.bbc.co.uk/1/hi/uk/2744443.stm (accessed 10 April 2008).

BBC Online (2 August 2001) 'Fears "keep children indoors"', London: BBC Online. Online. Available HTTP: http://news.bbc.co.uk/1/hi/education/1469600.stm (accessed 28 April 2008).

Beckford, M. (8 May 2007) 'School without play area bans break times', London: *Daily Telegraph*. Online. Available HTTP: http://www.telegraph.co.uk/news/uknews/1550808/School-without-play-area-bans-break-times.html (accessed 28 April 2008).

Bennett, R. (21 May 2007) 'Mum, get out of my Facebook: half of parents have turned into online spies', London: *Times*. Online. Available HTTP: http://technology.timesonline.co.uk/tol/news/tech_and_web/the_web/article1816570.ece (accessed 10 April 2008).

Benoit T. C., Jocelyn L. J., Moddemann D. M., and Embree J. E. (1996) 'Romanian adoption: the Manitoba experience', *Archives of Pediatric and Adolescent Medicine* 150: 1278–82.

Berndt, T. J. (1999) 'Friendships in adolescence', in M. Woodhead, D. Faulkner and K. Littleton (eds) *Making Sense of Social Development*, London: Routledge.

Blair, T. (21 November 2006) 'Tony Blair writes for *The Sun*', London: *Sun*. Online. Available HTTP: http://www.thesun.co.uk/sol/homepage/news/article72078.ece (accessed 10 April 2008).

Blatchford, P. (1999) 'The state of play in schools', in M. Woodhead, D. Faulkner and K. Littleton (eds), *Making Sense of Social Development*, London: Routledge.

Blatchford, P. (1998) 'Social life in school: pupils' experiences of playtime and recess from 7 to 16 years', *Journal of Research in Childhood Education* 11: 14–24.

BMA (British Medical Association) (2006) *Child and Adolescent Mental Health*, London: BMA.

Borland, S. (5 September 2007) 'Children to get happiness lessons in school', London: *Daily Telegraph*. Online. Available HTTP: http://www.telegraph.co.uk/news/uknews/1562117/Children-to-get-happiness-lessons-in-school.html (accessed 10 April 2008).

Boulton, M. J. (1994) 'Playful and aggressive fighting in the middle school playground', in P. Blatchford and S. Sharp (eds) *Breaktime and the*

School: Understanding and changing Playground Behaviour, London: Routledge.

Boulton, M. J. (1992) 'Rough physical play in adolescence: does it serve a dominance function?' *Early Education and Development* 3: 312–33.

Boulton, M. J., and Smith, P. K. (1990) 'Affective biases in children's perceptions of dominance relationships', *Child Development* 61: 221–9.

Bowlby, J. (1969) *Attachment and Loss* I, *Attachment*, London: Penguin Books.

Boyd, D. (2007) 'Why youth (heart) social network sites: the role of networked publics in teenage social life', in D. Buckingham (ed.) *Youth, Identity, and Digital Media*, MacArthur Foundation Series on Digital Learning, Cambridge MA: MIT Press.

Boyd, D. (2006) 'Identity Production in a Networked Culture: Why Youth Heart MySpace', paper presented at American Association for the Advancement of Science, St Louis, February.

Bristow, J. (29 August 2007) 'Having children can be good for you – and society', Spiked, London. Online. Available HTTP: http://www.spiked-online.com/index.php?/site/article/3768 (accessed 10 April 2008).

Bristow, J. (4 September 2002) 'Treating teachers like paedophiles', Spiked, London. Online. Available HTTP: http://www.spiked-online.com/Printable/00000006DA0F.htm (accessed 10 April 2008).

Brooks, L. (2006) *The Story of Childhood: Growing up in Modern Britain*, London: Bloomsbury.

Bruer, J. (1999) *The Myth of the First Three Years: A New Understanding of early Brain Development and Lifelong Learning*, New York: Free Press.

Bryson, B. (2007) *The Life and Times of the Thunderbolt Kid: Travels through my Childhood*, London: Black Swan.

Buckingham, D. (2005) 'Constructing the media competentchild: media literacy and regulatory policy in the UK', Median Padagogik. Online. Available HTTP: http://www.medienpaed.com/05–1/buckingham05–1.pdf (accessed 10 April 2008).

Byron, T. (2008) *Safer Children in a Digital World: The Report of the Byron Review*, London: DCSF.

CAPT (Child Accident Prevention Trust) (2002) *Taking Chances: the Lifestyles and Leisure Risk of Young People*, London: CAPT. Online. Available HTTP: http://www.capt.org.uk/pdfs/capt_risk_doc.pdf (accessed 10 April 2008).

Children's Society (26 February 2008) 'Concerns over commercialisation of childhood', London: Children's Society. Online. Available HTTP: http://www.childrenssociety.org.uk/whats_happening/media_office/latest_news/6486_news.html (accessed 10 April 2008).

Children's Society (2007) *The Good Childhood Inquiry*, London: Children's Society. Online. Available: HTTP: http://www.childrenssociety.org.uk (accessed 10 April 2008).

ChildWise (2007) *Monitor Trends Report*, Norwich: ChildWise. Online. Available HTTP: http://www.childwise.co.uk/trends.htm (accessed 11 April 2008).

Christakis, D. A., *et al.* (2004) 'Early television exposure and subsequent attentional problems in children', *Pediatrics* 113 (4): 708–13.

Clark, L. (11 October 2007), 'Children being robbed of their innocence by "guns, gangs and celebrities"', London: *Daily Mail*. Online. Available HTTP: http://www.dailymail.co.uk/pages/live/articles/news/news.html?in_article_id=487168&in_page_id=1770 (accessed 10 April 2008).

Clements, D. (4 October 2007) 'Every parent matters?' London: Spiked. Online. Available HTTP: http://www.spiked-online.com/index.php?/site/article/3928/ (accessed 10 April 2008).

Clements, R. (2004) 'An investigation of the status of outdoor play', *Contemporary Issues in Early Childhood* 5 (1): 68–80.

Clinton, H. (4 February 1997) 'Remarks by the President and the First Lady at White House conference on early child development and learning'. Online. Available HTTP: http://www.ed.gov/PressReleases/04-1997/970417d.html (accessed 10 April 2008).

Clinton, H. (1996) *It Takes a Village: and other Lessons Children teach us*, New York: Simon & Schuster.

Cockburn, A. (2006) 'Speaking at the launch of the Sense about Science report "Making Sense of Chemical Stories"', January.

Corsaro, W. A. (1999) 'Preadolescent peer culture', in M. Woodhead, D. Faulkner and K. Littleton (eds) *Making Sense of Social Development*, London: Routledge.

Coughlan, S. (5 June 2007) 'Why are we such worried parents?' BBC Online. Online. Available HTTP: http://news.bbc.co.uk/1/hi/education/6722225.stm (accessed 10 April 2008).

Crain, W. (2004) *Reclaiming Childhood: Letting Children be Children in our Achievement-oriented Society*, New York: Holt Paperbacks.

Cunningham, H. (2006) *The Invention of Childhood*, London: BBC Books.

DCSF (Department for Children, Schools and Families) (2008) 'Don't suffer in silence' web site. Available HTTP: http://www.dfes.gov.uk/bullying/ (accessed 13 June 2008).

DCSF (2007a) *The Children's Plan: Building Brighter Futures*, London: DCSF.

DCSF (2007b) *Staying Safe*, London: DCSF.

DCSF (2007c) *Confident, Capable and Creative: Supporting Boys' Achievements*, London: DCSF.

DfES (Department for Education and Skills) (13 March 2007) '"Getting the Best Possible Start": the Early Years Foundation Stage published today', London: DfES. Online. Available HTTP: http://www.dfes.gov.uk/pns/DisplayPN.cgi?pn_id=2007_0042 (accessed 10 April 2008)

DfES (2007) *Early Years Foundation Stage: Setting the Standards for Development, Learning and Care of all Children from Birth to the Age of Five*, London: DfES.

DfES (2006) *Safeguarding Children and Safer Recruitment in Education*, London: DfES.

DfES (2003) *Every Child Matters*, London: DfES.

DfES (2001) 'Guidance after the events of 11 September', London: DfES. Online. Available HTTP http://www.dfes.gov.uk/sept11guidance/ (accessed 10 April 2008)

DfT (Department for Transport) (2007) *National Travel Survey 2006*, London: Transport Statistics.

Directgov (15 March 2007) 'Department for Education and Skills recognises "Every Parent Matters"', London: DfES. Online. Available HTTP http://www.direct.gov.uk/en/Nl1/Newsroom/DG_066880 (accessed 10 April 2008)

Ecclestone, K., and Hayes, D. (2008) *The Dangerous Rise of Therapeutic Education*, London: Routledge.

Elkind, D. (2007) *The Power of Play: How Imaginative, Spontaneous Activities lead to Healthier and Happier Children*, Cambridge: Da Capo Lifelong Books.

Elkind, D. (2001) *The Hurried Child: Growing up too Fast too Soon*, Cambridge: Da Capo Press.

Evans, D (31 December 2007) 'Boys and their toys', *Guardian*. Online. Available HTTP: http://commentisfree.guardian.co.uk/dylan_evans/2007/12/boys_and_their_toys.html (accessed 10 April 2008).

Farmer, C., and Trikha, S. (2005) *2003 Home Office Citizenship Survey: Top-level Findings from the Children and Young People Survey*, London: Home Office and DfES.

Feinmann, J. (23 October 2007) 'Obesity "epidemic": who are you calling fat?', London: *Independent*. Online. Available HTTP: http://www.independent.co.uk/life-style/health-and-wellbeing/health-news/obesity-epidemic-who-are-you-calling-fat-397647.html (accessed 10 April 2008).

Feldman, S., and Marks, V. (2006) *Panic Nation: Unpicking the Myths we're Told about Food and Health*, London: John Blake.

FEMA (Federal Emergency Management Agency) (2001) 'How to talk to children about the threat of biological warfare or terrorist attack', Washington: FEMA, Online. Available HTTP: http://www.fema.gov/kids/terrism.htm (accessed 10 April 2008).

Fitzpatrick, J. (May 2007) 'Losing your sense of self', London: Spiked. Online. Available HTTP: http://www.spiked-online.com/index.php?/debates/article/3385/ (accessed 10 April 2008).

Flegal, K., *et al.* (2005) 'Excess deaths associated with underweight, overweight, and obesity', *Journal of the American Medical Association (JAMA)* 293: 1861–7.

Foresight (2007) *Tackling Obesities: Future Choices*, London: Department of Innovation Universities and Skills.

Frean, A. (12 October 2007) 'Pressure of tests "means primary school pupils lose their childhood"', London: *Times*. Online. Available HTTP: http://www. timesonline.co.uk/tol/life_and_style/education/article2641983.ece (accessed 10 April 2008).

Freud, S. (1908) *Creative Writers and Day-dreaming*, SE 9: 143–53.

FSA (Food Standards Agency) (6 September 2007) 'Chronic and acute effects of artificial colourings and preservatives on children's behaviour', London: FSA. Online. Available HTTP: http://www.food.gov.uk/science/research/ researchinfo/foodcomponentsresearch/allergyresearch/t07programme/t07proj ectlist/t07040/ (accessed 10 April 2008).

FSA (11 September 2007) 'Agency revises advice on certain artificial colours', London: FSA. Online. Available HTTP: http://www.food.gov.uk/news/ newsarchive/2007/sep/foodcolours (accessed 10 April 2008).

Furedi, F. (2007) 'Hijacking education', in F. Furedi *et al.* (eds) *The Corruption of the Curriculum*, London: Civitas.

Furedi, F. (9 November 2006) 'Adults behaving badly', London: Spiked. Online. Available HTTP: http://www.spiked-online.com/index.php?/site/ article/2077/ (accessed 10 April 2008).

Furedi, F. (2001) *Paranoid Parenting: Abandon your Anxieties and be a Good Parent*, Harmondsworth: Allen Lane.

Furedi, F. (1997) *Culture of Fear: Risk Taking and the Morality of Low Expectations*, London: Cassell.

Furedi, F., and Lewis, N. (2009) *Children's Real Digital World*, London: Futures Diagnosis.

Furstenberg, F., Rumbaut, R., and Settersten R. (2005) 'On the frontier of adulthood: emerging themes and new directions', in R. Settersten, F. Furstenberg and R. Rumbaut (eds), *On the Frontier of Adulthood: Theory, Research, and Public Policy*, Chicago: University of Chicago Press.

Future Foundation (2006) *The Changing Face of Parenting*, London: Future Fondation.

Gantz, W., Schwartz, N., Angelini, J. R., and Rideout, V. (2007) *Food for Thought: Television Food Advertising to Children in the United States*, Menlo Park CA: Kaiser Family Foundation.

Garner, R. (12 October 2007) 'The primary cause for concern', London: *Independent*. Online. Available HTTP: http://www.independent.co.uk/ news/education/education-news/the-primary-cause-for-concern-396669.html (accessed 10 April 2008).

Gerhardt, S. (2004) *Why Love Matters: How Affection Shapes a Baby's Brain*, Hove: Brunner-Routledge.

Gill, T. (2007) *No Fear: Growing up in a Risk-averse Society*, London: Gulbenkian Foundation.

Gill, T. (2006) 'Childhood freedoms and adult fears: growing up in a risk-averse society', *Alfredians* 4: 5–8.

Gill, T. (13 April 2005) 'Licence and confrontation', London: *Guardian*. Online. Available HTTP: http://education.guardian.co.uk/schools/comment/story/0,1458292,00.html (accessed 10 April 2008).

Ginsburg, K. (2007) 'The importance of play in promoting healthy child development and maintaining strong parent–child bonds', *Pediatrics* 119 (1): 182–91.

Goodchild, S. (2007) 'Advertisers and the commercialisation of childhood', *The Edge* 26: 14–15.

Grenier, J. (3 December 2002) 'Playing safe', London: Spiked. Online. Available HTTP: http://www.spiked-online.com/Printable/00000006DB6E.htm (accessed 10 April 2008).

Guldberg, H. (2007) 'A childish panic about the next generation' London: Spiked Review of Books, August issue. Online. Available HTTP: http://www.spiked-online.com/index.php?/site/reviewofbooks_article/3756/ (accessed 10 April 2008).

GYI (Generation Youth Issues) (26 November 2007) 'Cotton wool kids can't swim: the death of common sense?' Glasgow: GYI. Online. Available HTTP: http://www.generationyouthissues.org.uk/campaigns/swimming/cotton%20wool%20kids%20can't%20swim.htm (accessed 11 April 2008).

Hallam, S., Rhamie, J., and Shaw, J. (2006) *Evaluation of the Primary Behaviour and Attendance Pilot*, London: DfES. Online. Available HTTP: http://www.dfes.go.uk/research (accessed 10 April 2008).

Hardyment, C. (24 December 2007) 'Avoid the nursery wars', London: *Times*. Online. Available HTTP: http://women.timesonline.co.uk/tol/life_and_style/women/families/article3090331.ece (accessed 10 April 2008).

Harker, L., and Kendall, L. (2003) *An Equal Start: Improving Support during Pregnancy and the first Twelve Months*, London: IPPR.

Harris, J. R. (1999) *The Nurture Assumption: Why Children turn out the Way they Do*, New York: Free Press.

Hawkes, N. (6 September 2007) 'So which E-numbers should parents banish from their shopping basket?' London: *Times*. Online. Available HTTP: http://women.timesonline.co.uk/tol/life_and_style/women/diet_and_fitness/article2395611.ece (accessed 10 April 2008).

Health Committee (26 May 2004) 'Obesity report published', London: Department of Health. Online. Available HTTP: http://www.parliament.uk/parliamentary_committees/health_committee/hc260504_22.cfm (accessed 10 April 2008).

Healy, D. (2005) 'Psychopharmacology in Turmoil: an Ethical or Scientific Crisis?' Paper presented at a seminar graduate programme at Columbia University School of Public Health, New York, October.

Healy, D. (2004) *Let them eat Prozac: The Unhealthy Relationship between the Pharmaceutical Industry and Depression*, New York: NYU Press.

Hill, E. (9 February 2007) 'Is breast milk a "junk food"?' London: Spiked. Online. Available HTTP: http://www.spiked-online.com/index.php?/site/article/2837/ (accessed 10 April 2008).

Hillman, M., Adams, J., and Whitelegg, J. (1990) *One False Move: A Study of Children's Independent Mobility*, London: Policy Studies Institute.

High, B. (ed.) (2007) *Bullycide in America: Moms Speak out about the Bullying/suicide Connection*, Rocky Mountain House AB: JBS Publishing.

Hobson, P. (2004) *The Cradle of Thought: Exploring the Origins of Thinking*, London: Macmillan.

Hughes, B. (13 November 2006) Speech at the National Family and Parenting Institute conference 'Happy Families?'.

Hume, M. (14 June 2007) 'Castrate this sick debate', London: Spiked. Online. Available HTTP: http://www.spiked-online.com/index.php?/site/article/3483/ (accessed 10 April 2008).

Humphries, S., and Gordon, P. (1993) *A Labour of Love: the Experience of Parenthood in Britain. 1900–1950*, London: Sidgwick & Jackson.

Huxley, A. (1977) *Brave New World*, repr. London: Flamingo.

IPPR (Institute of Public Policy Research) (26 July 2007) 'Britain's poorest teenagers must be targeted by Government Youth Review', London: IPPR. Online. Available HTTP: http://www.ippr.org/pressreleases/?id=2811 (accessed 11 April 2008)

IPPR (6 November 2006) 'Britain's teenagers' social skills gap widens', London: IPPR. Online. Available HTTP: http://www.ippr.org/pressreleases/?id=2415 (accessed 11 April 2008)

IPPR (2 November 2006) 'Marriage promotion not the solution to "kids these days"', London: IPPR. Online. Available HTTP: http://www.ippr.org.uk/pressreleases/?id=2410 (accessed 10 April 2008)

James, O. (2002) *They F*** You Up: How to Survive Family Life*, Polmont: Bloomsbury.

James, O. (1998) *Britain on the Couch: Why we're Unhappier compared with 1950, Despite being Richer – A Treatment for the Low-serotonin Society*, London: Arrow Books.

Johnson, C. (20 February 2007) 'Among rich countries, US child well-being poor, but optimism prevails', Washington DC: OneWorld.net. Online. Available: HTTP: http://us.oneworld.net/article/view/146372/1/ (accessed 10 April 2008).

Johnston, P. (15 February 2007) 'Crisis point over Britain's disaffected youth', London: *Daily Telegraph*. Online. Available HTTP: http://www.

telegraph.co.uk/news/main.jhtml?xml=/news/2007/02/15/nkids15.xml (accessed 10 April 2008).

Jones, D. (2007) *Cotton Wool Kids: Releasing the Potential for Children to take Risks and Innovate*, Coventry: HTI.

Jones, W. K. (2006) *Different Times: a View of Life in inner Manchester during the First Decades of the Twentieth Century*, Sandy: Bright Pen.

Laming, Lord (2003) *The Victoria Climbié Inquiry*, Norwich: HMSO.

Lancy, D. F. (2007) 'Accounting for variability in mother–child play', *American Anthropologist* 109 (2): 273–84.

Lane, C. (2007) *Shyness: How Normal Behaviour became a Sickness*, New Haven CT: Yale University Press.

Layard, R. (2007) 'The Teaching of Values', Ashby Lecture presented at University of Cambridge, May.

Layard, R. (2007) 'Happiness and the teaching of values', *Centrepiece* 12 (1): 18–23.

Layard, R. (2005) *Happiness: Lessons from a New Science*, London: Allen Lane.

Lenhart, A., and Madden, M. (2007) *Social Networking Websites and Teens*, Washington DC: Pew Internet & American Life Project.

Levine, M. (2006) *The Price of Privilege: How Parental Pressure and Material Advantage are creating a Generation of Disconnected and Unhappy Kids*, New York: HarperCollins.

Lewis, N. (19 May 2008) 'To see the future of the internet, look East', London: Spiked. Online. Available HTTP: http://www.spiked-online.com/index.php?/site/article/5166/ (accessed 22 May 2008).

Linn, S. (2004) *Consuming Kids: The Hostile Takeover of Childhood*, New York: New Press.

Lipsett (11 December 2007) 'Teachers: we can't correct all society's ills', London: *Guardian*. Online. Available HTTP: http://education.guardian.co.uk/policy/story/0,2225351,00.html (accessed 11 April 2008).

Livingstone, S. (2005) 'Assessing the research base for the policy debate over the effects of food advertising to children', *International Journal of Advertising* 24 (3): 273–96.

Livingstone, S., and Bober, M. (2005) *UK Children go Online: Final Report of Key Project Findings*, London: LSE.

Livingstone, S., and Bovill, M. (1999) 'Young People, New Media: Report of the Research Project: Children, Young People and the Changing Media Environment', London: LSE.

Louv, R. (2005) *Last Child in the Woods: Saving our Children from Nature-deficit Disorder*, Chapel Hill NC: Algonquin Books.

Lyons, R. (17 October 2007) 'The dangers of fried food and a fried planet', London: Spiked. Online. Available HTTP: http://www.spiked-online.com/index.php?/site/article/3975/ (accessed 11 April 2008).

McDermott, N. (July 2007) 'Parents take parenting far too seriously', London: Spiked. Online. Available HTTP: http://www.spiked-online.com/index.php?/site/reviewofbooks_article/3630/ (accessed 11 April 2008).

Marano, H. E. (2005) 'Rocking the cradle of class', *Psychology Today*, September–October.

Marano, H. E. (2004) 'A nation of wimps', *Psychology Today*, November–December.

Margo, J., et al. (2006) *Freedom's Orphans: Raising Youth in a Changing World*, London: IPPR.

Marsh, J., et al. (2005) 'Digital beginnings: young children's use of popular culture, media and new technologies', Sheffield: Literacy Research Centre University of Sheffield. Online. Available HTTP: http://www.digitalbeginnings.shef.ac.uk/DigitalBeginningsReport.pdf (accessed 11 April 2008).

Marsh, P. (22 May 2005) 'An epidemic of confusion', Oxford: Social Issues Research Centre. Online. Available HTTP: http://www.sirc.org/obesity/epidemic_of_confusion.shtml (accessed 11 April 2008).

Marshall, S. J., et al. (2004) 'Relationships between media use, body fatness and physical activity in children and youth: a meta-analysis', *International Journal of Obesity* 28: 1238–46.

Marx, K. (1983) *Capital: a Critique of Political Economy* I, London: Lawrence & Wishart.

Mathews, J. (2 October 2001) 'Cancelling school trips is a bit extreme', Washington DC: *Washington Post*.

Mayo, E. (2006) 'The boundaries of protections', in 'RU TXTng 2 me? Young people, mobiles and social networking', London: Spiked/O2 online debate. Online. Available HTTP: http://www.spiked-online.com/index.php?/debates/C95/ (accessed 11 April 2008).

Mayo, E. (2005) *Shopping Generation*, London: National Consumer Council.

Meikle, J. (14 April 2007) 'Sharp rise in pupils suspended for racism', London: *Guardian*. Online. Available HTTP: http://education.guardian.co.uk/raceinschools/story/0,2056792,00.html (accessed 11 April 2008).

Meikle, J. (13 April 2007) 'Rise in number of pupils suspended for racial abuse', London: *Guardian*. Online. Available HTTP: http://www.guardian.co.uk/uk/2007/apr/14/race.schools (accessed 11 April 2008).

Meiklem, P. J. (24 October 2004) 'Mixed messages on raising children plunge parents into confidence', Glasgow: *Sunday Herald*.

Mercogliano, C. (2007) *In Defense of Childhood: Protecting Kids' Inner Wildness*, Boston MA: Beacon Press.

Midgley, C. (26 June 2007) 'Young and desperate', London: *Times*. Online. Available HTTP: http://women.timesonline.co.uk/tol/life_and_style/women/families/article1983887.ece (accessed 11 April 2008).

Miles, A., and Rumbelow, H. (4 August 2007) 'How many adults does it take to let children play outside?' London: *Times*. Online. Available HTTP: http://www.timesonline.co.uk/tol/news/uk/article2195532.ece (accessed 11 April 2008).

Mintz, S. (2006) *Huck's Raft: A History of American Childhood*, Cambridge MA: Harvard University Press.

Morrison, B. (6 February 2003) 'Life after James', London: *Guardian*. Online. Available HTTP: http://www.guardian.co.uk/uk/2003/feb/06/bulger.ukcrime (accessed 11 April 2008).

Morrison, B. (1997) *As if*, London: Granta Books.

Nansel, T. R., Overpeck, M., Pilla, R. S., Ruan, W. J., Simons-Morton, B., and Scheidt, P. (2001) 'Bullying behaviors among US youth', *JAMA* 285: 2094–100.

National Centre for Social Research, Department of Epidemiology and Public Health at the Royal Free and University College Medical School (2004) *Health Survey for England, 2003*, London: Department of Health.

National Playing Fields Association (2000) *Best Play: what Play Provision should do for Children*, London: NPFA.

NCC (National Consumer Council) (8 July 2005) 'Children call for controls on marketing and action on rip-offs in landmark Shopping Generation study', London: NCC. Online. Available HTTP: http://www.ncc.org.uk/news_press/pr.php?recordID=325&PHPSESSID=17542e72d8093274bbfcc6e1a190d888 (accessed 15 May 2008).

News.com.au (15 May 2007) 'Bullied boy receives record $1 m payout', Sydney: News Digital Media. Online. Available HTTP: http://www.news.com.au/story/0,23599,21730222-2,00.html (accessed 15 May 2008).

NSKC (National Safe Kids Campaign) (2003) *Report to the Nation: Trends in Unintentional Childhood Injury Mortality, 1987–2000*, Washington DC: NSKC.

NSPCC (National Society for the Prevention of Cruelty to Children) (15 May 2006) 'NSPCC launches "Don't hide it" sex abuse campaign as rape reports to ChildLine reach new high', London: NSPCC. Online. Available HTTP: http://www.nspcc.org.uk/whatwedo/mediacentre/press-releases/15_may_2006_nspccdont_hide_it_launch_wdn33556.html (accessed 15 May 2008).

NUT (National Union of Teachers) (2001) *Terrorist Attacks – Advice from the National Union of Teachers*, London: NUT.

OfCom (Office of Communications) (2008) *Social Networking: A Quantitative and Qualitative Research Report into Attitudes, Behaviours and Use*, London: OfCom.

Oliver, C., and Candappa, M. (2003) *Tackling Bullying: Listening to the Views of Children and Young People*, London: DfES.

O'Neill, B. (27 October 2006) 'A crude Act that will poison young minds', London: *Catholic Herald*.

O'Neill, B. (3 October 2005) 'Is junk food a myth?' London: BBC Online. Online. Available HTTP: http://news.bbc.co.uk/1/hi/magazine/4304118.stm (accessed 11 April 2008).

Opie, I. (1993) *The People in the Playground*, Oxford: Oxford University Press.

Opie, I., and Opie, P. (1959) *Lore and Language of Schoolchildren*, Oxford: Clarendon Press.

Palmer, S. (2007) *Detoxing Childhood: What Parents Need to Know to Raise Happy, Successful Children*, London: Orion.

Palmer, S. (27 July 2007) 'Youth clubs won't tame the teenage yobs', *Daily Telegraph*, London. Online. Available HTTP: http://www.telegraph.co.uk/portal/main.jhtml?xml=/portal/2007/07/27/nosplit/ft-teens-127.xml (accessed 10 April 2008).

Palmer, S. (2006) *Toxic Childhood: How the Modern World is Damaging our Children and What we Can Do about It*, London: Orion.

Parson, S. (26 November 2007) 'Teens2: introducing our editors', London: *Times*. Online. Available HTTP: http://women.timesonline.co.uk/tol/life_and_style/women/the_way_we_live/article2933864.ece (accessed 11 April 2008).

Paul, P. (21 November 2007) 'Tutors for toddlers', New York: *Time*. Online. Available HTTP: http://www.time.com/time/magazine/article/0,9171,1686826,00.html (accessed 11 April 2008).

Pellegrini, A. (2005) *Recess: Its Role in Education and Development*, Mahwah NJ: Erlbaum.

Pellegrini, A., and Blatchford, P. (2000) *The Child at School: Interactions with Peers and Teachers*, London: Edward Arnold.

Piaget, J. (2002) *The Language and Thought of the Child*, repr. London: Routledge Classics.

Piaget, J. (1977) *Moral Judgement of the Child*, repr. London: Penguin Education Books.

Piaget, J. (1962) *Play, Dreams and Imitation in Childhood*, repr. New York: Norton Library.

Piper, H., Powell, J., and Smith, H. (2006) 'Parents, professionals, and paranoia: the touching of children in a culture of fear', *Journal of Social Work* 6 (2): 151–67.

Plumb, J. H. (1971) 'The great change in children', *Horizon* 13 (1): 4–12.

Pooley, C. (2006) *A Mobile Century? Changes in Everyday Mobility in Britain in the Twentieth Century*, Aldershot: Ashgate Publishing.

Postman, N. (1994) *The Disappearance of Childhood*, New York: Vintage Books.

Primary Review (2007) *Community Soundings: the Primary Review Regional Witness Sessions*, Cambridge: University of Cambridge Faculty of Education.

Purves, L. (11 December 2007) 'Stand up for Nicky No-names', London: *Times*. Online. Available HTTP: http://www.timesonline.co.uk/tol/comment/columnists/libby_purves/article3031200.ece (accessed 11 April 2008).

Purves, L. (8 May 2007) 'How did we learn to be so defeatist?' London: *Times*. Online. Available HTTP: http://www.timesonline.co.uk/tol/comment/columnists/libby_purves/article1760011.ece (accessed 11 April 2008).

Quart, A. (2006a) *Hothouse Kids: How the Pressure to Succeed is Threatening Childhood*, London: Arrow Books.

Quart, A. (2006b) 'Extreme parenting', *Atlantic Monthly* 298 (1): 21–4.

Reuters (14 October 2007) 'Obesity crisis could be "on par with climate change"', London: Reuters. Online. Available HTTP: http://uk.reuters.com/article/domesticNews/idUKL1433848220071014 (accessed 11 April 2008).

Rideout, V. J., Vandewater, E. A., and Wartella, E. A. (2003) *Zero to Six: Electronic Media in the Lives of Infants, Toddlers and Preschoolers*, Menlo Park CA: Kaiser Family Foundation.

Roberts, D. F., Foehr, U. G., and Rideout, V. (2005) *Generation M: Media in the Lives of 8–18 Year-olds*, Menlo Park CA: Kaiser Family Foundation.

Rooney, K. (29 October 2007) 'Citizenship education: making kids conform', London: *spiked*. Online. Available HTTP: http://www.spiked-online.com/index.php?/site/article/4023/ (accessed 11 April 2008)

Rousseau, J-J. (1979) *Émile*, repr. New York: Basic Books.

RoSPA (Royal Society for the Prevention of Accidents) (2007) *Review 06:07*, Birmingham: RoSPA.

Rutter, M. (1998) 'Developmental catch-up and deficit following adoption after severe global early privation', *Journal of Child Psychology and Psychiatry* 39: 465–76.

Schaffer, R. H. (2004) *Introducing Child Psychology*, Oxford: Blackwell.

Schaffer, R. H. (2000) 'The early experience assumption: past, present, and future', *International Journal of Behavioral Development* 24: 5–14.

Schaffer, R. H. (1996) *Social Development*, Oxford: Blackwell.

Schor, J. B. (2004) *Born to Buy: The Commercialized Child and the New Consumer Culture*, New York: Scribner.

Sense about Science (2006) *Making Sense of Chemical Stories*, London: Sense about Science.

Settersten, R., Furstenberg, F., and Rumbaut, R. (2005), *On the Frontier of Adulthood: Theory, Research, and Public Policy*, Chicago: University of Chicago Press.

Shea, C. (15 July 2007) 'Leave those kids alone', Boston MA: *Boston Globe*. Online. Available HTTP: http://www.boston.com/news/globe/ideas/articles/2007/07/15/leave_those_kids_alone/ (accessed 15 May 2008).

SIRC (Social Issues Research Centre) (2007) *Girl Talk: The New Rules of Female Friendship and Communication*, Oxford: SIRC.

Skenazy, L. (9 June 2008) 'Why you shouldn't over-protect your kids', London: *Times*. Online. Available HTTP: http://women.timesonline.co.uk/tol/life_and_style/women/families/article4095977.ece (accessed 13 June 2008).

Skenazy, L. (1 April 2008) 'Why I let my nine-year-old ride the subway alone', New York: *New York Sun*. Online. Available HTTP: http://www.nysun.com/opinion/why-i-let-my-9-year-old-ride-subway-alone/73976/ (accessed 13 June 2008).

Sky News (13 October 2007) 'Safety bosses bonkers about conkers', London: Sky News. Online. Available HTTP: http://news.sky.com/skynews/article/0,30100–1288276,00.html (accessed 11 April 2008)

Sonkin, B. (2006) 'Walking, cycling and transport safety: an analysis of child road deaths', *Journal of Royal Society of Medicine* 99: 402–5.

Stearn, P. (2003) *Anxious Parents: a History of Modern Childrearing in America*, New York: NYU Press.

Taylor, M., *et al.* (2004) 'The characteristics and correlates of fantasy in school-age children: imaginary companions, impersonation, and social understanding', *Developmental Psychology* 40: 1173–87.

Taylor, M. (2001) *Imaginary Companions and the Children who Create Them*, New York: Oxford University Press.

Taylor, M. (2000) 'Of Hobbes and Harvey: the Imaginary Companions created by Children and Adults', paper presented at the University of Oregon, January.

Thomas, G., and Thompson, G. (2004) *A Child's Place*, London: Demos/Green Alliance.

Thompson, R. A., Lamb, M. E., and Estes, D. (1982) 'Stability of infant–mother attachment and its relationship to changing life circumstances in an unselected middle-class sample', *Child Development* 53: 144–8.

Timimi, S. (2004) 'Rethinking childhood depression', *British Medical Journal* 329: 1394–6.

Ungar, M. (2007) *Too Safe for their own Good: How Risk and Responsibility help Teens Thrive*, Toronto: McClelland & Stewart.

UNICEF (2007) *Child Poverty in Perspective: An Overview of Child Well-being in Rich Countries*, Innocenti Report Card 7, Florence: Innocenti Research Centre.

UNICEF (2001) *A League Table of Child Death by Injury in Rich Nations*, Innocenti Report Card 2, Florence: Innocenti Research Centre.

University of Chicago Press (2008) 'On the frontier of adulthood: Theory, Research, and Public Policy publicity page'. Online. Available HTTP: http://www.press.uchicago.edu/cgi-bin/hfs.cgi/00/16467.ctl (accessed 15 May 2008).

University of Washington News (2004) 'Two-thirds of school-age children have an imaginary companion by age seven', Washington DC: University

of Washington. Online. Available HTTP: http://www.uwnews.org/article.
asp?articleID=6814 (accessed 15 May 2008).

Vygotsky, L. S. (1986) *Thought and Language*, Cambridge MA: MIT Press.

Vygotsky, L. S. (1978) *Mind in Society: Development of Higher Psychological Processes*, Cambridge MA: Harvard University Press.

Waiton, S. (27 July 2007) 'Young children are being short-changed', London: *Times Education Supplement (TES)*. Online. Available HTTP: http://www.tes.co.uk/search/story/?story_id=2414453 (accessed 11 April 2008).

Waters, E. (1978) 'The reliability and stability of individual differences in infant–mother attachment', *Child Development* 49: 483–94.

Webster, B. (11 September 2007) 'Careful parents may cost lives', London: *Times*. Online. Available HTTP: http://news.sky.com/skynews/article/0,30100–1288276,00.html (accessed 11 April 2008).

Wessely, S. (1998) 'Britain on the couch: treating a low-serotonin society', *British Medical Journal* 316: 83.

WHO (World Health Organization) (2005) *Mental Health: Facing the Challenges, Building Solutions: Report from the WHO European Ministerial Conference*, Copenhagen: WHO.

WHO (2001) *Mental Health: New Understanding, New Hope*, Geneva: WHO.

Woods, R. (20 May 2007) 'Watch with mother', London: *Sunday Times*. Online. Available HTTP: http://www.timesonline.co.uk/tol/news/uk/article 1813498.ece (accessed 11 April 2008).

Zaslow, J. (6 September 2007), 'Avoiding kids: how men cope with being cast as predators', New York: *Wall Street Journal*.

Zaslow, J. (23 August, 2007), 'Are we teaching kids to be fearful of men?', New York: *Wall Street Journal*.

Zelizer, V. (1994) *Pricing the Priceless Child: The Changing Social Value of Children*, Princeton NJ: Princeton University Press.

INDEX

accidents 14, 60–61, 66–67; *see also* road accidents
additives 29–31
ADHD *see* Attention Deficit Hyperactivity Disorder
adults: children as distinct from 48, 49–50, 51, 54–55; emotional engagement with children 145; Europe 14; guidance from 90, 91; impact of traumatic events on children 101; lack of sanctions by 177–78; men 171–72; playground supervision 64–65; role models 10; solidarity 170–71; suspicion towards 165, 166–68, 169–70, 171–72, 179–80; *see also* parents
adventure 70
advertising 7, 112, 113, 114; children's perception of 115–16; food 29, 114–15
aggression 84, 86, 109
Aigner-Clark, Julie 38
Ainsworth, Mary 133–34
alcohol use 9, 14, 15, 175
Alexander, Robin 23

American Academy of Child and Adolescent Psychiatry (AACAP) 160
American Academy of Pediatrics (AAP) 81–82, 83, 120
American Psychiatric Association 21
American Psychological Association (APA) 113
Anderegg, David 71–72, 84–85, 136, 144
Anti-Bullying Alliance (ABA) 95
anti-depressants 18, 19
antisocial behaviour 15, 152, 163, 175
anxiety 17, 22; bullying 100; parental 69, 85; policymakers 40; shyness 21–22; *see also* fears; worry
Appleton, Josie 165
Arens, Ursula 31
Aries, Philippe 47, 49
Armstrong, Aaron 93
attachment theory 133–34, 136
Attention Deficit Hyperactivity Disorder (ADHD) 30, 117, 120–21

Auerbach, Stevanne 141
avoidant personality disorder 21–22

Baby Einstein 37–38, 82
Bailey, Donald 135
Bailey, Sue 20
Balls, Ed 65, 111–12, 124–25, 139,
    151
Basham, Patrick 26, 27
'battery children' 10–11, 33–34
Beat Bullying 97
Bentham, Jeremy 157
Berndt, Thomas 87
Big Brothers Big Sisters 172
binge-drinking 9, 17
Blair, Tony 129, 139, 141
Blatchford, Peter 107, 109
Bober, Magdalena 122
Boulton, Michael 109
Bovill, Moira 120
Bowlby, John 133
Boyd, Danah 124, 126
boys 83–84, 109
brands 112, 114
break time 107
Bristow, Jennie 89–90, 156
British Medical Association (BMA)
    19
Brooks, Libby 12, 88, 92, 143
Brown, Gordon 26
Brucia, Carlie 175
Bruer, John 135
Bryson, Bill 44
Buckingham, David 25, 115–16
Building Brighter Futures 65, 94, 156
Bulger, James 55
bullying 7, 17, 55, 88, 92–110, 163;
    cyberbullying 96–97, 98, 99,
    124–25; dealing with 100–101;
    fear of 42; media reports 175;
    racist incidents 102–4
BullyingUK 95

Bush, George W. 38, 83
Byron, Tanya 125

Campaign for Commercial-free
    Childhood 113
Carlson, Stephanie 76–77
Carr, John 97
celebrity 22
Centre for Analysis of Social
    Exclusion (CASE) 113
Chapman, Jessica 175
child abuse 137–39, 140, 156,
    168–69, 172
Child Accident Prevention Trust
    (CAPT) 42–43
child labour 51–52, 53
Child Welfare League of America
    (CWLA) 11
ChildLine 95, 169, 175
Children Act (2004) 139
Children and Nature Network 9
Children's Plan 65, 94, 111, 139,
    151–52
Children's Play Council 33, 36, 42,
    108
Children's Society 11;
    commercialism 113; friendship
    87; outdoor play 36, 42; parental
    fears 10, 32–33; play 85–86
Christakis, Dimitri 120–21
Clements, David 140
Clements, Rhonda 35, 107
Climbié, Victoria 137, 138, 140
Clinton, Hillary 9, 129–30
Cockburn, Andrew 31
cognitive development 76, 149
commercialism 9, 111–12, 113–14,
    115
common sense 67, 140, 146, 160
Community Soundings (Primary
    Review 2007) 8–9, 22–24, 149–51,
    152–53

computer games 7, 120
conflict 87, 99, 108, 110
conkers 61–62
consumerism 12, 112, 114, 116
Corsaro, William 108
Cox, Benjamin 100–101
Crain, William 82
crime 55–56
Crime and Disorder Act (1998) 55
Criminal Records Bureau (CRB) 156, 165
Cunningham, Hugh 47–48
cyberbullying 96–97, 98, 99, 124–25

'dangerous places' 43
death 14, 47, 60–61, 66, 68
Delap, Miles 106
Demos 42, 163, 164
Department for Children, Schools and Families (DCSF) 19, 83, 94, 96–97
Department for Education and Skills (DfES) 19, 156, 158, 159
depression 8, 17, 18, 22; BMA report 19; bullying 100; diagnosis 20
developing countries 53–54
Diagnostic and Statistical Manual of Mental Disorders (DSM) 21–22
Dingle, Ceri 53
doom-mongering 11–12, 24, 175, 180
drug use 9, 15, 175
Dunford, John 152

Early Years Foundation Stage (EYFS) 39, 83, 148–49
eating disorders 18
Ecclestone, Kathryn 154–55
Economic and Social Research Council (ESRC) 112–13

education 13, 48, 50, 51, 54; government targets 83; 'happiness classes' 153–55; infants 37–38, 82; National Curriculum 107, 147, 148; No Child Left Behind Act 147–48; Zone of Proximal Development 90; see also schools; teachers
Education Act (1870) 51
egocentrism 77
Einstein, Albert 147
Elkind, David 9, 37, 45, 89, 114, 116
emotional deprivation 136–37
emotional disorders 19–20
emotional engagements 145
emotional skills 153–55
emotions 75, 101, 109
Enlightenment 49, 51
Europe 9–10, 13, 14–16, 177
Every Child Matters 139, 140, 151
exam pressure 22, 23, 24; see also testing
extracurricular activities 39, 89

Facebook 17, 124
failure, experience of 45, 69
family breakdown 22, 23
fantasy 9, 74–75, 76, 82
Fass, Paula 177
fatness see obesity
fears: children's 42–43, 163–64; culture of fear 170; of men 171–72; parental 10–11, 32–33, 162–63, 175; projection of adult fears on to children 25, 180; of strangers 164–65; see also anxiety; worry
fights 14, 104–6
Fitzpatrick, John 89
Flemmen, Asbjørn 64
food: additives 29–31; advertising 29, 114–15; obesity 25–29

Food Standards Agency (FSA) 29, 30
Fowlie, Lisa 62
free time 37
freedom 10–11, 32–33, 59, 70–71, 79
Freud, Sigmund 74–75
friends 85–88, 91, 108; online communication 123–24; time spent with 10, 14–15
Furedi, Frank 12, 117, 152, 170–71, 177–78
Future Foundation 16, 43

games 54
gangs 17
Generation Youth Issues 41–42, 102, 163
Gerhardt, Sue 130, 133, 140–41
Ghana 53–54
Gifford, Rob 69
Gill, Tim 63, 64, 108, 152, 161, 164–65, 166
Go4it initiative 62
The Good Childhood Inquiry: commercialism 113; friendship 87, 88; parental fears 10, 32; play 85–86
government intervention: culture of mistrust 176; education 148, 150, 153, 156, 159–60; parenting 139–41, 142–43; scaremongering 175
government targets 38–39, 83, 131–32, 149
Green, Al Aynsley 11
Green Alliance 42, 163
Greenaway, Mike 62
Grenier, Julian 41
guidance 90, 91
guns 83–84, 85

Hallam, Susan 154
Hampden Gurney Primary School 40

Hannibal 53
happiness 8, 18–19, 153–55
Hardyment, Christina 144
Harris, Judith Rich 131
Hart, Adrian 102–4
Hawkes, Nigel 30
Hayes, Dennis 154–55
health: food additives 29–31; obesity 25–29; television impact on 120–21
health and safety 40, 41, 61–62, 64, 66
Health and Safety Executive (HSE) 61–62
Healy, David 20
'helicopter parents' 89, 174
Hewitt, Alistair 158
High, Brenda 93
Hill, Emily 29
Hobson, Peter 145
'hothousing' 38–39, 82
Hughes, Beverley 141, 142, 149
Hume, Mick 176
hyperactivity 30
hyper-parenting 89

identity 87, 90
imaginary friends 76–77
imaginary play 9, 73–74, 75, 76, 78–79, 80–81, 82
industrial revolution 52
infant determinism 129–37, 145, 146
Institute for Public Policy Research (IPPR) 9, 10, 14–16, 39, 112, 177
Institution of Occupational Safety and Health (IOSH) 62
internet 17, 111, 122–26; cyberbullying 96–97, 98, 99, 124–25; surveillance 44
Ishaq, Khyra 138–39

James, Oliver 130–32, 133
Johnson, Alan 26, 139
Jones, Digby 62–63
Jones, William Kenneth 82–83
'junk culture' 8
'junk food' 8, 29

Kaiser Family Foundation 114, 118, 119
Kanka, Megan 175
Knight, Jim 97
Knight, Simon 163
Koocher, Gerald 113–14
Koonce, Mack 172

Lancy, David 141–42
Lane, Christopher 21–22
Larkin, Philip 130
Layard, Richard 153–54, 155
learning: child-centred 90; from experience 45
legislation: Children Act 139; Crime and Disorder Act 55; Education Act 51; No Child Left Behind Act 83, 147–48; Safeguarding Vulnerable Groups Act 165, 175
Levine, Madeline 17
Lewis, Norman 117, 123
life expectancy 27, 28, 31
Linn, Susan 113
Livingstone, Sonia 44, 114–15, 120, 122
Locke, John 50
Louv, Richard 9, 34
Luik, John 26

Major, John 55
make-believe 73–74, 78–79, 81
Manifesto Club 165
Marano, Hara Estroff 69
Marks, Vincent 29
Marsh, J. 119

Marsh, Mary 138, 169
Marx, Karl 28, 51–52
Mathews, Jay 159
Mayo, Ed 114, 123
McCann, Madeleine 175, 176
mealtimes 16
media 8–9, 26, 113, 115, 117–21, 175; see also television
men 167, 171–72
mental health 8, 15, 17–22, 131
Mercogliano, Chris 7, 33, 37, 41, 89, 117–18, 122
Middle Ages 47–49
Midgley, Carol 18
Mintz, Steven 12, 32, 45, 46, 47, 53
MMR vaccine 67
mobile phones 97, 98
morality 79
Morgan, Mary 143–44
Morrison, Blake 55–56
'Mosquito' device 163
Mullarkey, Tom 60, 61
MySpace 17, 124, 126

National Academy for Parenting Practitioners 141
National Bullying Survey 95
National Consumer Council (NCC) 112, 114, 123
National Curriculum 107, 147, 148
National Institute of Child Health and Human Development (NICHD) 94, 96
National Society for the Prevention of Cruelty to Children (NSPCC) 137, 168–69, 175
National Union of Teachers (NUT) 160
'nature deficit disorder' 9, 34
NCH 8, 20
Netmums 30
neuroscience 134–36

No Child Left Behind Act (2001) 83, 147–48
Norway 1, 59, 60, 64
nostalgia 7, 23
nurseries 38–39, 43

obesity 25–29, 114, 121, 152, 175
Olweus, Dan 95–96
O'Neill, Brendan 165–66
Opie, Iona 105–6, 108
optimism 24
oral communication 49
outdoor play 10–11, 32–36, 44; children's fears about 42, 163; Norway 1, 59, 60; television impact on 119–20
overprotectiveness 17, 32, 42, 67, 70, 151, 179

paedophiles 2, 162, 165, 170; 'awareness campaigns' 176; internet 124–25; media reports 175, 176; men's fear of being labelled as 167, 171, 172; photographs of children 168
Palmer, Sue 8, 10, 25–26, 33, 130
panics 12
Parentline Plus 44
parents 2, 129–46; accident prevention 67; attachment theory 133–34; bullying 97; commercial pressures on 116–17; *Community Soundings* 23; confidence 141, 142–44; fears 10–11, 32–33, 162–63, 175; freedom given to children 70–71, 172–74, 175; hyper-parenting 89; insecurities 12; lack of faith in 40; parent-child play 141–42; parenting industry 2, 140–42; pre-school educational programmes 37–38; schools' role 152; surveillance of children's internet use by 44; suspicion of other adults 179–80; teachers' view of 152–53; time spent with children 10, 15–16; trusting children's choices 72; weapons play 84; Wilde on 129; worries about children 43, 84–85, 142, 144; *see also* adults
Parson, Sandra 17
Pasteur, Louis 72
Payne, Sarah 175
Pearce, Nick 10, 14
peer pressure 15, 87–88
Pellegrini, Anthony 86, 107
pessimism 24
Petersen, Steve 135
photographs 167–68, 170
Piachaud, David 112
Piaget, Jean 73, 74, 77, 78, 79, 149
Pinker, Steven 130–31
Piper, Heather 157
play 8, 9, 33, 45, 73–85, 91; barriers to 81–83; boys 83–84; decline in time allowed for 37; friendship 88; importance of 110; parent-child 141–42; playground safety 63–65; pre-school children 73–74, 75, 77–83; risk-taking 62; self-directed 39, 83; Zone of Proximal Development 90; *see also* outdoor play
Play England 176–77
Playday 162
play-fighting 34, 85, 109
playgrounds: banning of traditional games 40; behavioural codes 93; bullying 94, 106–7; fun 108; rough-and-tumble play 109; safety panics 63–65
Plumb, John 49
political correctness 103

Pooley, Colin 36
Postman, Neil 46, 47, 48–49, 50, 54–55
poverty 13
pre-school children: educational programmes 37–38, 82; media impact on 118–21; play 73–74, 75, 77–83
Primary Review 2007 (*Community Soundings*) 8–9, 22–24, 149–51, 152–53
privacy 43–44, 88–89, 91
problem solving 90
Programme of International Student Assessment (PISA) 13
Purves, Libby 106–7, 118

Quart, Alissa 37–38

racism 55, 102–4
Read the Signs 18
Reid, John 176
Reitemeier, Bob 11, 42
respect 12, 23
responsibility 70–71
Rhodes, Laura 93
risk 34, 40, 61, 62–63; child protection 138–39; children's perception of 42–43; emotional 92; online communication 125–26; playground panics 63–65; road crossing 68, 69
road accidents 67–69
role models 10
Romanian orphanages 136–37
Romanticism 50
Rooney, Kevin 151
rough-and-tumble play 85, 109
Rousseau, Jean-Jacques 50–51
Royal Society for the Prevention of Accidents (RoSPA) 60, 61, 67
rules 79

Safeguarding Vulnerable Groups Act (2006) 165, 175
safety 2, 12, 63–65, 66; see also health and safety
Schaffer, Rudolph 101, 134, 136
schools: bullying 94, 106–7; Children's Plan 151–52; fights 104–6; 'happiness classes' 153–55; playground games bans 40; racist incidents 102–4; risk aversion 62; suspicion towards adults 156–58; see also education; teachers
Schor, Juliet 114
self-discovery 32, 88
self-harm 15, 18
Seligman, Martin 153
September 11th terrorist attacks 158–60
sex 9, 12, 14
sex education 152
shyness 21–22
Sinnott, Steve 149–50
Skenazy, Lenore 173–74
Social and Emotional Aspects of Learning (SEAL) programme 153–55
social anxiety 21–22
Social Issues Research Centre (SIRC) 27
social networking sites 122, 123, 124, 125
social skills 153–55
socialization 11, 40, 78, 126, 151, 177
Somerville, Julia 167
Sparks, Ian 33
Spears, Linda 11
special needs 21
spiked 2, 29, 89, 123, 151, 156, 165
Spock, Benjamin 143–44
sports 35, 37
St John's Primary School 40

'statementing' of children 21
Stearn, Peter 40
'Strange Situation' test 133–34
strangers 2, 161–62, 164–66, 170, 176
streets 34, 36, 43, 163, 176–77
stress 8–9, 22, 24, 150
structured lives 36–39, 83
suicide 18, 93
'superhero play' 83–84
'super-nannies' 141
supervision 37, 43–44, 45, 64–65, 162
surveillance 43–44, 88, 157
suspicion 165, 166–68, 169–70, 179–80; of men 171–72; of teachers 156–58
swimming pools 41, 167–68
Sylvan Learning Systems 38
symbolic play 73–74
Szasz, Thomas 59

Taylor, Marjorie 76
teachers 2, 90, 147–60; bullying 94, 98–99; exams 24; racist incidents 102–4; September 11th terrorist attacks 158–60; suspicion towards 156–58; see also education; schools
teasing 108, 109
Teather, Sarah 103
technology: adult anxieties 12; cyberbullying 96–97, 99; media landscape 111; surveillance 43, 44; see also internet
teenagers 9–10, 180; freedom given to 71; friends 14–15, 87–88; internet use 123–25; unhappiness 19
television 7, 9, 54, 111, 118–20; downward trend in children's viewing 122, 123; impact on

health 120–21; 'junk food' advertising 29; reality TV 17; see also media
terrorism 158–60, 163
testing 7, 8, 24, 90, 147–48, 150; see also exam pressure
Thailand 53
'Theory of Mind' 77–78
Thomas Coram Research Unit 94–95
Thomas Deacon city academy 106
Timimi, Sami 20
touching children 157
toys 9, 82, 83–84, 116
traffic dangers 42, 67–69, 163–64
traumatic events 101
Troedsson, Hans 17–18

Ungar, Michael 56, 67, 70, 171
UNICEF: accidental deaths 61; health and safety 66; road accidents 67–68; unhappiness 8; well-being report 11, 12–14, 23
United States: accidental deaths 14, 60–61, 66; bleak view of childhood 9; break time 107; bullying 94; commercialism 113–14; Hannibal 53; No Child Left Behind Act 83, 147–48; outdoor play 35, 37; parent-child play 142; playgrounds 64–65; poverty 13; pre-school educational programmes 37–38; social networking sites 124; surveillance 43; television 119; UNICEF report 11

violence 9, 14; murders 55, 175; school fights 104–6; see also child abuse
Voce, Adrian 176–77
Vygotsky, Lev Semenovich 73, 76, 78–79, 80–81, 90

Wadge, Andrew 30
Waiton, Stuart 41–42, 102
water 31
'weapons play' 83–84, 85
well-being 11, 66; friendship influence on 87; school initiatives to promote 154–55; UNICEF league table 12–14
Wells, Holly 175
Wessely, Simon 131
Wilde, Oscar 129
Wolf, Maryanne 38
Woods, Richard 44

World Health Organization (WHO) 17–18, 22
Worldwrite 53
worry 67, 84–85, 142, 144; *see also* anxiety; fears

Yearly, David 61

Zaslow, Jeffrey 171–72
Zelizer, Viviana 48
Zone of Proximal Development (ZPD) 90